EDINBURGH

in your pocket

D1390277

MAIN CONTRIBUTOR: PAUL MURPHY

PHOTOGRAPH CREDITS
Photos supplied by The Travel Library:
front cover, back cover, 4-5, 9, 17, 22, 48, 54, 68, 83,
86, 88, 92, 94, 97, 102, 110, 122; Roger Howard 25,
36, 43, 56, 70, 78, 87, 113; Sam Howard 21, 33, 46,
90; David McGill 64; Jonathan Smith 6-7, 8, 10, 18,
27, 28, 29, 30, 31, 32, 34, 37, 38, 40, 41, 42, 44-45,
47, 49, 50, 51, 52, 53, 60, 61, 62, 67, 72, 74, 76, 80,
81, 82, 85, 100, 101, 104, 105, 106, 107, 109, 115,
117, 125, 126.
Other Photos:
National Gallery of Scotland, Edinburgh/
Bridgeman Art Library 13; Private Collection/The
Stapleton Collection/Bridgeman Art Library 16;
Paul Murphy title page, 26, 59, 66, 73, 75, 120.

*Front cover: Edinburgh Castle, seen from Grassmarket;
back cover: Douglas Stewart Memorial, with Edinburgh
beyond; title page: bagpiper*

MANUFACTURE FRANÇAISE DES PNEUMATIQUES MICHELIN

Place des Carmes-Déchaux – 63000 Clermont-Ferrand (France)

© Michelin et Cie. Propriétaires-Éditeurs 2002

Dépôt légal Jan 02 – ISBN 2-06-100056-8 – ISSN 1272-1689

No part of this publication may be reproduced in any form

without the prior permission of the publisher.

Printed in Spain 01/02

MICHELIN TRAVEL PUBLICATIONS
Hannay House
39 Clarendon Road
WATFORD Herts WD17 1JA - UK
☎ (01923) 205240
www.ViaMichelin.com

MICHELIN TRAVEL PUBLICATIONS
Michelin North America
One Parkway South
GREENVILLE, SC 29615
☎ 1-800 423-0485
www.ViaMichelin.com

CONTENTS

INTRODUCTION

'There are no stars so lovely as Edinburgh
street lamps,' wrote Robert Louis Stevenson
and, whichever way and whatever time of day
you view her, Edinburgh is one of Europe's
most beautiful cities. There's not another
capital which has a green swathe like Princes
Street Gardens running through its heart, nor
one that has a mini mountain like Arthur's Seat
right in the city centre; no other capital has so
many panoramic viewpoints or quirky ups and
downs. Her crag-top castle is the stuff of fairy
tales, while the dark narrow alleyways of the
Old Town and higgledy-piggledy buildings
along its half-hidden closes and alleyways
(wynds) are straight out of a period film set.

By contrast, down in the New Town all is
harmony and light. Only in Dublin and Bath
will you see such splendid Georgian terraces
and well-ordered circuses, while out in the
suburbs are neat and characterful villages and
unspoiled hills and countryside.

Most visitors think of Edinburgh as a small
place, which can be seen in a long weekend,

but it is easy to spend a couple of weeks here and still not tire of all that the city has to offer. Of course, everyone does the Castle-Princes Street-Royal Mile circuit but relatively few visitors walk up to Arthur's Seat, relax in the Botanic Gardens, enjoy the Scottish National Gallery of Modern Art, go as far as the Forth Bridges or even know about Rosslyn Chapel.

To make the choice even greater, Edinburgh in the third Millennium has some terrific new visitor attractions: the brilliant Our Dynamic Earth, which draws uncomfortable parallels with London's failed Dome; The Royal Yacht *Britannia*; and the new Parliament Buildings at Holyrood which will be the biggest treat of all for fans of modern architecture.

Happily, 21C Edinburgh is neither the tartan-shortbread theme park of Sir Walter Scott, nor so steeped in its own history that its future is stifled. Its many students and festivals ensure that it remains a vibrant young city, and its banking and service industries are in good shape. Now, with a modern Parliament in residence and so much going on for locals and visitors, the future for Edinburgh looks bright.

The beautiful city of Edinburgh, seen from Calton Hill.

BACKGROUND

GEOGRAPHY

Edinburgh lies some 32km (20 miles) inland from the east coast of Scotland and 88km (55 miles) north of the border with England. The city centre is less than 3km (2 miles) south of the broad estuary known as the Firth of Forth, and its port Leith. The Forth is visible from any vantage point in the Old Town, and on clear days makes a wonderful backdrop to the city.

Like Rome, Edinburgh is built on seven hills, though it may seem many more as you puff your way up and down. Three of these – Castle Rock, Arthur's Seat and Calton Hill – are right in the centre: the others – Corstophine Hill

(home to the Zoo), Blackford Hill (home to the Royal Observatory), Braid Hill and Wester Craiglockheart – are just a few minutes' bus ride away. The highest at 251m (823ft) is Arthur's Seat, like Castle Hill, an ancient volcanic plug. The smallest, at 100m (328ft), is Calton Hill. The views from all are well worth the climb.

The hilly, undulating nature of Edinburgh city centre and the viewpoints offered from all sorts of different angles and heights are what make it so interesting and picturesque. Linking one part of the city to the next are hundreds of steps and some spectacular bridges. This is one of the world's finest cities for walking, so make sure you bring comfortable shoes.

The dramatic volcanic landscape of Salisbury Crags overlooks the city centre.

HISTORY

Celts, Romans and Scots

It is thought that the earliest people in the area around Edinburgh were hunting tribes who settled some 5 000 years ago. By around 1000 BC, farmers and the Beaker People from Continental Europe had arrived. Warring **Celtic tribes**, driven out of England and Southern Europe, then occupied the country.

The nearest the **Romans** came, in around AD 78, was Cramond and Inveresk, both about 8km (5 miles) from the present city centre. They defeated the local chief, Calgacus The Swordsman, and imposed a peace of sorts until their departure in the second century.

During the Dark Ages, waves of Angles, Vikings, Britons, Celts and the eponymous **Scots** (from Western Ireland) fell upon the land. It is thought that it was the **Celts** who were the first tribe to rule from the Castle Rock, around AD 600, and who named it *Dun Edin* 'the hill fort of Edin'. During this period, Edinburgh lay just across the border from England and in 638 the **Northumbrians** conquered southern Scotland and fortified the Castle Rock.

This stained-glass window in St Margaret's Chapel, Edinburgh Castle, depicts Queen Margaret, Malcolm III's wife.

The Early Kings

The Northumbrians held Castle Rock for around 400 years, until King **Malcolm II** reclaimed the area for the Scots tribe and pushed south the border with England. His son, **Malcolm III**, built a hunting lodge on the rock where he lived with his saintly wife, **Margaret**. Their son, **David I**, built a chapel here in memory of Margaret, which still stands today (*see* p.25). By the early to middle 12C, David I had founded Holyrood Abbey and the town had its own mint. Around this time it was also granted the status of Royal Burgh, taking on its present name, *Edinburgh*.

Sir William Wallace, one of the legendary heroes of the Scottish nationalist movement.

The following two centuries were to be turbulent and confused, with much Scottish-English intermarrying and many different claims to the Scottish throne. **Edward I** of England was asked to arbitrate upon the matter and imposed **John Baliol** as a puppet king. In 1295, however, when Baliol was ordered to supply Edward with men and arms against England's old enemy, France, Baliol refused. Instead, he formed a pact with France which was to be maintained over the coming centuries and came to be known as the **Auld Alliance**. The enraged Edward occupied Edinburgh and Scotland with such brutality that he earned the nickname 'Hammer of the Scots'. Despite the struggle of national freedom fighters such as **William Wallace** (*see* p.87), the English held Scotland until 1314, when **Robert the Bruce** defeated Edward II at Bannockburn (*see* p.87) and the castle was retaken. Unfortunately, the peace treaty of 1328 counted for little; the two countries were soon at war again and remained so for the next three centuries.

The statue of Robert the Bruce at the Bannockburn Heritage Centre, Stirling marks the site of his command post prior to the battle.

The Medieval City

In 1349 the Black Death ravaged the city, reducing the population by a third; by 1376 the population of Edinburgh was only around 2 000, with 400 houses straggling down the hill from the castle. The **Old Town** began to take its present shape around the mid-15C; the first town wall was built and, with the patronage of the early Stuart kings, the city assumed the roles of royal residence and seat of

government. The Castle and the Kirk of
St Giles were the first major landmarks, and the
town's characteristic narrow alleyways (wynds)
and closes began to be formed.

During the reign of **James IV** (1473-1513)
there was a brief period of peace and
prosperity. James proved to be the most
popular and most able Scottish king in
memory, and under him Edinburgh developed
from wooden shacks to stone houses where
merchants and nobles lived. Along with court
patronage came a flowering of knowledge and
the arts, including the establishment of the
College of Surgeons (1505) and the first
printing press (1507).

Sadly, this brief Golden Age died along with
the king, some 10 000 soldiers and hundreds of
nobles, on the battlefield at **Flodden** in 1513. It
was the blackest day in Scotland's history. The
people of Edinburgh, fearing that the English
would arrive any day, prepared for a siege and
began to erect a new wall, the Flodden Wall
(which was not to be fully completed until
years after the battle, in 1560). This wall
marked the city limits for the next 200 years or
so. As the city was already overcrowded, the
only way it could grow was up. Over the coming
years, what has been described as Europe's first
skyscrapers, 'lands' (tenements) were built,
reaching up to 12, perhaps even 14 storeys
high, a sort of medieval Manhattan. The
inhabitants lived cheek by jowl in appallingly
claustrophobic conditions; the tall buildings
shut out nearly all sunlight; there was no
sewage system nor running water.

The English did come; they sacked
Holyroodhouse Palace, right outside the city
wall, but the defenders inside held firm. When
James V died in 1542, after his defeat at the
Battle of Solway, the country and capital were
once again thrown into turmoil.

Mary Queen of Scots

As James V lay dying in 1542, his daughter Mary was born at Linlithgow Palace, delivered into a hotbed of political and religious machinations. She became queen after just six days and was immediately a pawn of the Scottish lords. The pro-English faction wanted her to marry Edward, son of Henry VIII, but the Auld Alliance supporters favoured the French *dauphin*, François, and fearful for her life spirited her away to France.

In 1558, at the age of 15, Mary married into the French royal family. That same year the English queen, Mary Tudor, died, prompting the supporters of Mary Stuart to claim that their Mary was the legitimate successor to the English crown above her cousin Elizabeth, regarded by many as an illegitimate heir. It was a claim that Elizabeth did not forget.

In 1560, François died from illness and Mary returned home to Scotland. The poor, cold, bleak, trouble-torn country she returned to was a shock to her every sense. Moreover, in the 13 years Mary had been away, Scotland had turned Protestant.

In 1565 she fell in love with, and married, Lord Darnley. The political consequences were huge, for Darnley would become king of Scotland and, since he was a grandson of Mary Tudor, also strengthened Mary's claim to the throne of England. But Darnley was a vain, selfish man and became insanely jealous of her (platonic) relationship with her private secretary, David Rizzio. In March 1566 Darnley brutally murdered Rizzio at Holyroodhouse (*see* p.57). Three months later, Mary gave birth to their son, James.

Now estranged from Darnley, Mary turned to the Earl of Bothwell for help. In 1567 Darnley was strangled; Bothwell was charged with his murder, but he intimidated the city by bringing his army of 4 000 men to town and was acquitted. Soon afterwards, Mary scandalised the nation by marrying him.

Later that year Bothwell's ambitions were to be thwarted when his forces were confronted by a group of heavily armed Scottish nobles. Without bloodshed, he surrendered the Queen, who was imprisoned in Lochleven Castle and forced to abdicate in favour of her son, the future James VI.

Some ten months later, however, Mary managed to escape and join her loyal band of supporters. They were routed near Glasgow and Mary, inexplicably, chose to throw herself upon the mercy of her cousin, Elizabeth I.

Unsure what to do with this political hot potato, Elizabeth imprisoned Mary for 18 years without trial, never once meeting her. Then in 1586, to a background of mounting Catholic pressure against Elizabeth and plots to put Mary on her throne, Elizabeth's spies discovered letters from Mary plotting her cousin's assassination. In 1587 Mary was taken to Fotheringay Castle, tried for treason, convicted and beheaded.

The Return of Mary Queen of Scots to Edinburgh, *by James Drummond (National Gallery of Scotland, Edinburgh).*

The Union of the Crowns

After all the bloodshed of Mary's time, the reign of her son James was to be the longest period of peace (some 42 years) that Scotland and England had yet enjoyed. When Elizabeth I died in 1603, the Union of the Crowns between the two countries was sealed – James was proclaimed **James I of England** and **James VI of Scotland**. His court immediately moved to London. The royal palaces of Scotland went into decline and Edinburgh lost much of its pageantry and cultural activity.

In 1637 Anglo-Scottish relationships were once again strained as **Charles I** attempted to bring the Scottish church into line with the church in England. The following year, the **National Covenant** was drawn up and signed in Greyfriars Churchyard by those supporting the king but opposing his religious policy. The English Civil War proved a confusing distraction in this struggle. The king was defeated (and later executed) but the Scots had thrown in their lot with the Royalists and they too were beaten by Cromwell, whose forces occupied Edinburgh.

The restoration of **Charles II** meant the reintroduction of his father's religious policies. Revolts were soon put down and vicious recriminations taken against those who had signed the National Covenant. The following years became known as **The Killing Time**, with several hundred Covenanters executed, deported or simply left to die in squalid jail conditions.

In 1688, following the flight of James VII and the end of the Catholic Stuart dynasty, many in Edinburgh rejoiced but most Scots, particularly the Highlanders, were still **Jacobites** (i.e. supporters of James, *Jacobus* in Latin). The famous rebellion of 1745 saw **Bonnie Prince Charlie** briefly reinstalled at Holyroodhouse

Palace, but his ambitions to put the Stuart line back on the throne died on the battlefield of **Culloden** the following year.

Meanwhile, in 1707 the Scottish Parliament had been dissolved by the English in what was known as the **Treaty of Union**. In return, the English guaranteed the Scottish Presbyterian (Protestant) Kirk. The Scots did not have their own parliament again for nearly 300 years.

The Enlightenment

In contrast with the turmoil of the first part of the 18C, Edinburgh in the late 18C was to enjoy its **Golden Age**. Great men like the visionary George Drummond, architects James and Robert Adams, philosophers David Hume and Dugald Stewart, economist Adam Smith and 'the father of geology' James Hutton, helped the city to prosper and to break out of the straitjacket imposed by the Old Town, now bursting at the seams with 50 000 inhabitants. Scarcely a new house had been built outside the Old Town since Flodden, and living conditions were said to be the worst in all Europe.

The competition to design the **New Town** was won in 1766 by the 21-year-old James Craig. Nor'Loch, a foul lake which had covered the site of what is now Princes Street Gardens, was drained, the Mound was built and by the 1790s over 7 000 people had moved from Old to New. During this period, **Edinburgh University** blossomed into one of the finest in Europe; the arts also flourished, with painters such as Allen Ramsay and Henry Raeburn, and poets and novelists including **Robert Burns** and **Sir Walter Scott**, supported by the growth of famous literary magazines, publishers, printers and booksellers. The sobriquet **'Athens of the North'** applied to Edinburgh as a centre of learning as much as to its Greek Revival architecture.

Edinburgh's Men of Letters

Edinburgh has long held a great reputation as an erudite city and has produced two great writers: Sir Walter Scott and Robert Louis Stevenson.

Robert Louis Stevenson was born in 1850 at 8 Howard Place, North Edinburgh, moving at the age of seven to 17 Heriot Row in the New Town, the house which he immortalised in *The Lamplighter*, a poem from his charming classic collection, *A Child's Garden of Verses* (1885).

His first Edinburgh-based book was *Edinburgh, Picturesque Notes,* which is still very readable today. In 1880 he co-wrote *Deacon Brodie* (*see* p.32), perhaps as a prelude to his 1886 classic *The Strange Case of Dr Jekyll and Mr Hyde*.

Stevenson was an inveterate traveller throughout his life, spending much time abroad on account of his poor health. In 1883 came his first novel and most popular work, *Treasure Island*; in 1886 *Kidnapped* was published. The following year Stevenson left Edinburgh for the last time, emigrating to America. Ever the adventurer, he sailed the South Seas and bought a house on Samoa, where he settled with his family.

He championed the local cause against forced colonialism, was treated with great honour and became known as Tusitala ('Teller of Tales'); he stayed in Samoa until he died suddenly in 1894 from a cerebral haemorrhage.

Sir Walter Scott was born in 1771 in College Wynd (now demolished), off Cowgate. The family moved to 25 George Square, where Scott lived until 1797 when he married. He was

called to the Scottish Bar in 1792 but his love of romantic literature led in 1802-3 to his first publication, a collection of ballads entitled *The Minstrelsy of the Scottish Border*, which achieved great success. In 1804 he left Edinburgh for country life in Ettrick Forest. After more poems and more success, in 1812 he moved again to his beloved Abbotsford, in the Borders, and began his romantic 'Waverley' novels including *Waverley*, *Guy Mannering*, *Rob Roy* and *The Heart of Midlothian*. Their phenomenal success brought Scott a huge income. Now an international name, this fierce patriot gained even greater fame by petitioning successfully for 'The Honours of Scotland' to be found in Edinburgh Castle (*see* p.26). Created a baronet, he organised the historic visit of King George IV to Scotland in 1822 and, with his lavish overuse of archaic Highland Celtic imagery, especially tartan, he set the phoney romantic style for which Scotland is still known today (and for which also, in

many quarters, Scott is reviled).

By 1825, however, the printers and publishers, Ballantynes, in which Scott was a partner, had incurred massive debts. To repay his liabilities, he began five years of incessant writing, during which time his health deteriorated disastrously. Sir Walter Scott died at Abbotsford in 1832 and was buried nearby in Dryburgh Abbey.

Left: Robert Louis Stevenson.

Right: Sir Walter Scott's statue in the Scott Monument, Princes Street Gardens.

The Nineteenth Century

By the early 1800s much of the New Town was
complete and the city population had topped
100 000. Generally it was still only the wealthy
who could move from the squalor of the Old
Town, where cholera, alcoholism, fire and
collapsing buildings continued to take their
toll and lawlessness grew. Edinburgh had
become a city of two faces; Robert Louis
Stevenson's *Jekyll and Hyde* was a comment on
Edinburgh's own character as much as on the
historical persona of Deacon Brodie (*see* p.32)
– a case of 'fur coat and nae knickers', as the
locals still say today.

On the right side of the tracks, **Walter Scott**
hosted George IV's historic visit to Edinburgh
with so much tartan pomp and Highland
pageantry that it set a stereotype of Scotland
which still exists today (*see* p.17) . The **railways**

came and connected Edinburgh to London, the magnificent Forth Rail Bridge was built and the suburbs, including many neat and charming little villages, began to develop. Queen Victoria showed great affection for Scotland and Edinburgh, and in her wake came the first **tourists**. Victorian philanthropists and reformers began Charity Schools and the Temperance movement, and the Improvement Acts in 1867 at last began to strip away some of the Old Town slums.

Modern Times

Edinburgh city centre has changed relatively little in the last hundred years. Ignore the garish shopfronts from Princes Street and the view is more or less unchanged from the early 20C. In the Second World War the lack of heavy industry in Edinburgh saved it from the bombs, which fell instead on its port, Leith, and on Glasgow.

Although it may not have seemed so at the time, one of the most significant developments in the last century was the formation of the **Edinburgh Festival**, in 1947. Today it has become so large and spawned so many offshoots (*see* pp.94-95) that it is a year-round industry, which in 1995 was estimated to have generated almost £100 million of additional income for the city. It is also a vital and very visible flagship for the tourist industry, which now forms a significant part of the Edinburgh economy.

Undoubtedly the city's finest moment in recent times came on 1 July 1999, with the return of a **Scottish Parliament** to Edinburgh after an absence of almost 300 years. Its temporary home is the Assembly Hall, off the Royal Mile, but the impressive new 21C buildings at Holyrood eagerly await their new Millennium Scottish Parliamentary representatives.

A triumph of Victorian engineering – the Forth Rail Bridge (1890), South Queensferry.

PEOPLE AND CULTURE

One of the first things that a keen-eared visitor to Edinburgh will notice is the number of English and foreign accents in the city, and not just from fellow tourists. Many an English 'migrant' who now works in Edinburgh will tell you that the quality of life is so much higher here than in London or other parts of England.

Edinburgh has always been a cosmopolitan city; its great university and medical establishments attract students from all over the world, while in recent years the global nature of the International and Fringe Festivals has attracted many more overseas visitors and residents.

Less flattering is the old-fashioned image of Edinburgh folk ('Edinburghers') as dour and strait-laced, as exemplified by Miss Jean Brodie in the eponymous novel and film. The stereotype fits easily – just think well-to-do, tight-lipped, rather pretentious, living in the New Town or posher suburbs. The antithesis of this is the down-to-earth working-class Edinburgh lad (or lass) who enjoys companionship, probably revels in the poetry of Burns and is partial to a drink or two. It is a convenient pairing of caricatures that is played out for dramatic effect and a good number of laughs nightly on the Literary Pub Tour (*see* p.124) by 'Miss McBrain' and 'Mr Clart' – there are no prizes for guessing who represents which faction. Happily, after much banter and a few drinks, the two protagonists find quite a lot in common. It's a clever little parable on the famously dual persona of Edinburgh's citizens, though as a general rule the locals you meet will be welcoming, keen to help you and rarely have any recall to airs, graces or false ('have a nice day') bonhomie.

One thing that does unite all Edinburgh folk is their love of Scotland. Edinburgh may have a reputation for being Anglophile, or at the very least for being less aggressively patriotic than some other Scottish cities – Glasgow, for example – but that doesn't mean its inhabitants are any less committed to the 'Blue Blanket' (the flag of St Andrew). It's a good point to remember when the subject of football or politics comes up in the pub – as it surely will!

Life in Edinburgh, as in every other modern city, is imperfect. Begging, usually of the peaceful and passive kind, is prevalent on the streets and at pub closing time it is best to avoid places like the Grassmarket, where groups of booze-fuelled youths (not necessarily from Edinburgh, it must be said) can be unpleasant. On the whole, however, Edinburgh city centre is peaceful and safe, night and day.

Once the site of public hangings, today the Grassmarket is one of Edinburgh's most attractive squares.

MUST SEE

Edinburgh Castle★★
Your eyes will be drawn to it, from every angle, so curiosity alone demands a visit. Inside, there's 800 years of history, great views and a very good audio tour to enjoy.

Holyrood Park
When the sun shines and the east wind relents, climb the Salisbury Crags, wind your way round, then up to **Arthur's Seat** for the splendid **panorama★★**. Finish off a perfect morning or afternoon with a drink in the Sheep's Heid, at Duddingston. Don't forget your camera.

Our Dynamic Earth
Be there at the Big Bang, really feel the earth move, touch an iceberg, catch a shower in the tropical rainforest and learn the

Brooding Edinburgh Castle looks out over Princes Street Gardens.

story of our constantly changing planet from such authoritative sources as the BBC and National Geographic, while moving through a series of state-of-the-art 'earthscapes'.

Princes Street Gardens

Pull up a deckchair and listen to the band, let the kids off the leash, have an ice-cream, gaze up at the castle or just watch the world go by. For a bird's-eye view of it all, climb the **Scott Monument★**. In summer, there's not a prettier city park anywhere in the world.

National Gallery of Scotland★★

The perfect spot to shelter from the rain or for a cultural break from the shopping hordes of Princes Street. Many of the Old Masters are represented here. When you feel you are overdosing on the richness of Renaissance Italy, seek out the great French Impressionists.

Charlotte Square★★★

You don't need to be an architectural expert to recognise that this is the epitome of Georgian town-planning. The **Georgian House★** is a little on the dry side but don't miss coffee at nNumber 28. Walk out of the square along George Street for more New Town elegance.

Royal Museum and Museum of Scotland★★★

These two adjoining collections are the perfect foil for each other: cutting-edge displays on all things Scottish in the former, a magpie's nest of world treasures in the latter. Dip into each at will.

Royal Yacht *Britannia*★

For visitors of a certain age, this is the ultimate nostalgia trip. A brilliant introductory exhibition whets the appetite, with fascinating fly-on-the-wall facts and trivia before you actually tread the hallowed decks.

Scottish National Gallery of Modern Art★

Not sure about modern art? This gallery and its sister, **Dean Gallery★** across the road, have converted many a sceptic. Both are bright, breezy, inventive and witty, with excellent cafés (on a sunny day choose the SNGMA for its patio).

Forth Bridges★★

Take a trip to South Queensferry and you will be in little doubt why, 110 years ago, they called the Forth Rail Bridge the Eighth Wonder of the World. Compare its over-engineered specification with the sleek and suspended but equally strong Forth Road Bridge.

THE ROYAL MILE

The Royal Mile – so named because it stretches for one mile between the Castle and Holyroodhouse Palace – is the historic heart of Edinburgh. Sandwiched between these two great Scottish institutions are several museums and historic houses open to the public, whisky and weaving centres, St Giles' Cathedral, haunted underground streets and dozens of eating, drinking and shopping establishments. By night, the dim narrow alleyways which lead off the Mile conjure up dark, medieval images.

The Royal Mile is, in fact, just over a mile in length, and its different sections are named (in descending order): Castlehill, Lawnmarket, High Street, Canongate and finally, Abbey Strand.
(Note: Holyroodhouse Palace is featured under *Holyrood and Calton Hill, see* p.55)

Edinburgh Castle★★
Perched high above the city on its great grey basalt crag, the castle is almost as potent a symbol today as it was in centuries past. As early as the 11C it was a royal residence, although the oldest part of the present castle dates from the early 12C. It began to assume its present form from about 1650 onwards. Included in the ticket price is an excellent audio tour.

Head straight to the top of the castle for great **views★★** over Princes Street and the New

Edinburgh Castle dominates the city, set up high on a rocky outcrop.

Watching and waiting by the One O'Clock Gun. No matter how ready you think you are, the explosion will still make you jump!

Town. At 1pm every day, except Sunday, the famous **One O'Clock Gun** booms out from here. This was originally a time signal for the shipping below and the signal has been fired ever since 1861, except during the World Wars. Just above, on the highest part of the castle, is **St Margaret's Chapel**, the oldest building, dedicated by King David I to his mother, Queen Margaret, some time after 1250.

The Royal Palace complex was built in the second half of the 15C. Today much of it is devoted to an exhibition which traces the

history of Scotland's royal regalia – the **Honours of Scotland★★★**; this is some of the oldest regalia in the world (predating the British Crown Jewels in London) and is beautifully displayed under subdued lighting. Here too is the legendary **Stone of Scone**, also known as the Stone of Destiny, upon which ancient Scottish kings were enthroned. It was seized by Edward I in 1296 and remained for 700 years (more or less) as part of the Coronation Chair in Westminster Abbey, until it was returned to Scotland in 1996.

Highlights of the Royal Apartments are the **Great Hall** and **Queen Mary's Chambers**, where Mary Queen of Scots resided briefly in 1566 to give birth to the future king, James VI of Scotland (James I of England). The former has the finest interior in the castle, famous for its splendid **hammerbeam roof★★**.

Below the Great Hall are the **vaults**, or dungeons, where prisoners were confined (albeit in relatively civilised conditions) in the 18C and 19C. The most famous 'resident' today is **Mons Meg**, one of the two largest siege guns

Follow the process from start to finish at the Tartan Weaving Mill and Exhibition.

ever built, capable of firing a devastating 150kg (330lb) cannonball over 3km (2 miles). Opposite the Royal Palace is the atmospheric **Scottish National War Memorial**, a huge sombre hall, converted in mock-medieval baronial fashion in 1923 to honour the nation's fallen.

Other exhibitions in the castle grounds which will appeal to militarily-inclined visitors are the **National War Museum**, the **Royal Scots Museum** and the **Royal Scots Greys Museum**.

Castlehill and Lawnmarket

Immediately below the Castle Esplanade, the twin Scottish icons of whisky and tartan have been turned into visitor attractions. Despite its tacky entrance, it is worth persevering with the **Tartan Weaving Mill and Exhibition**, if only to see the tartan weaving looms in action. These are not simply demonstration or museum pieces but real, everyday noisy production machinery. Ask one of the helpful, well-informed guides to explain the process and give you a go on a pedal-powered loom.

Call in at the Camera Obscura for a sneak view of the city and her inhabitants.

The Hub stairwell, decorated with striking red statues, provides a suitably dramatic entrance to the Festival Centre.

Opposite, the **Scotch Whisky Heritage Centre** is a much more polished affair. It welcomes visitors with a wee dram, before a short film and a large-scale distillery model provide the didactic part of the tour. The Blender's Ghost and the Whisky Barrel ride add hokum to the story.

If the castle hasn't already satisfied your appetite for panoramic views, pop into the **Outlook Tower** and test out the **Camera Obscura**, where the art of large-scale pinhole photography has been delighting visitors since 1853. Holograms and other new-fangled optical tricks have their own galleries but the ability to 'spy' on passers-by over a wide area is the real appeal here. It's obviously best to visit on a clear day.

Towering taller than all else in Edinburgh – even the castle – is the blackened spire of the old **Tolbooth Church**, at 73m (240ft). It was built in 1844, abandoned in 1984, then re-opened in 1999, after being given a stunning interior makeover by the Edinburgh Festival organisers. Today it is known as **The Hub,** and functions as Festival offices, concert hall, sculpture exhibition, café (*see* pp.104-5), restaurant and shop. The bold and beautiful use of tiling, colour, sculptures and modern fittings to complement the old church interior makes it an attraction in its own right. Next to The Hub, running off the Mile, **Victoria Street★** is Edinburgh's quaintest shopping street (*see* p.110).

Curved, cobbled and very picturesque, Victoria Street provides a charming link between the Grassmarket and George IV Bridge.

Back on the other side of the road, easily missed, off Milne's Court, is the entrance to the (temporary) **Scottish Parliament Debating Chamber**. It was here in the imposing historic Assembly Hall, built in 1858-9 for the General Assembly of the Free Church of Scotland, that the Scottish Parliament first reconvened in July 1999, after a lapse of 300 years (*see* p.19), and where members will continue to sit until about May 2003 when they take up their places in the new Holyrood Building. Meetings are open to the public (normally Wednesday afternoons and Thursday all day). Tickets are free but must be requested, no more than a week in advance (☎ **0131 348 5411**). The chamber is also usually open Mondays and Fridays and all weekdays during recess periods, 10am-noon and 2-4pm. For more details, visit the **Scottish Parliament Visitor Centre**, on the corner of the Royal Mile and George IV Bridge.

The Assembly Hall, temporary home of the Scottish Parliament, seen here from Princes Street Gardens.

At the Assembly Hall, the Royal Mile broadens out into the stretch known as **Lawnmarket**, once the setting for a linen market. The most characteristic architectural feature of Edinburgh's Old Town is its towering tenement (apartment) blocks, known in the ancient vernacular as 'lands'. **Gladstone's Land★**, measuring a comparatively modest six storeys and with an original arcaded frontage and painted interiors dating from the 17C, is the best surviving example of such a building. It is now administered by the National Trust for Scotland and its enthusiastic staff tell the story of its several atmospheric rooms (*closed Nov-Mar*).

Gladstone's Land is one of Edinburgh's finest tenement buildings.

Just off the Lawnmarket, **Lady Stair's Close** is one of the most picturesque of Edinburgh's closes, with tall handsome buildings enclosing a couple of tiny squares, including the popular Jolly Judge pub (*see* p.103). **Lady Stair's House** was built in 1622 and, although much renovated, provides an atmospheric mock-Jacobean home for the **Writers' Museum**. A floor is dedicated to each of Scotland's great literary triumvirate: Robert Louis Stevenson (*see* p.16), Sir Walter Scott (*see* p.17) and Robert Burns, with rare collections of memorabilia and manuscripts (*closed* Sun).

The Writers' Museum sign.

On the corner of Lawnmarket and Bank Street, the **Deacon Brodie** pub celebrates one of the city's most famous characters. William Brodie, an eminently respectable cabinet-maker, town councillor and deacon (president) of the Edinburgh Wrights and Masons guild, led a double life: by night he became a gambler, womaniser and – to pay for his massive debts – an armed robber. He was hanged in 1788, supposedly on a new scaffold trapdoor mechanism of his own design. It is claimed by some that his double life was the inspiration for Stevenson's Jekyll and Hyde.

Of more interest than the pub is **The Deacon's House** (now a café), in Brodie's Close opposite. This was the home of Brodie's father, Francis, and the arched kitchen is a 15C survivor of his cabinet-making workshop. Murals on the café wall (and the friendly owner, if he has the time) tell the story of his infamous son, who for a time also lived here.

High Street

At the crossroads with George IV Bridge and
Bank Street, Lawnmarket ends and the High
Street section of the Mile begins. Immediately
on the right is **Parliament Square**, with the
Georgian façade of Parliament Hall to the
south, but dominating it all in the centre of the
square is **St Giles' Cathedral****. Its open crown
spire** is one of Edinburgh's most famous

*Soot-blackened
St Giles' Cathedral,
with its distinctive
crown spire.*

landmarks. Just before the cathedral's entrance, look down onto the cobbled street to see the **Heart of Midlothian**, a heart-shaped arrangement of setts (stone blocks). It marks the site of the old tollbooth, which stood here from the late 14C to 1817. It had many functions, most notoriously as a prison, named the Heart of Midlothian in the eponymous novel by Sir Walter Scott. Many a rogue was hanged outside the prison at this spot, including Deacon Brodie. Today, Scots spit on the heart for good luck.

The cathedral, also known as the High Kirk of Edinburgh, was built in its present form in 1385, though the four piers supporting the tower remain from the previous 12C church.

This stained glass window in St Giles' Cathedral depicts John Knox preaching at the funeral of the Earl of Moray, murdered at Linlithgow.

Alterations and restorations have, however, radically altered its late medieval character. **John Knox**, whose statue stands in the nave, was its most famous minister (1560-1572) and the leader of the Scottish Reformation. The highlight of the church is the Flamboyant Gothic style **Thistle Chapel**, designed in 1911 and dedicated to Scotland's Order of Chivalry. The carving of the stalls, canopies and bosses is of the highest craftsmanship – look up to see if you can spot the angel playing the bagpipes. Other points of interest include the rather incongruous bright, large, modern organ (1992), and two literary memorials; near the entrance (to the right) is Robert Louis Stevenson in classic reclining pose, while the modern abstract design in the west window (1984) relates to the life and works of Robert Burns (ask a church warden to help you decipher it!).

Behind the cathedral, next to the 17C equestrian statue of Charles II, are the Supreme Courts of Scotland. The public may attend cases, or simply look in to see the splendid **Parliament Hall** where, from 1639 to 1707, the Scottish Parliament met beneath its striking hammerbeam roof (*Mon-Fri 9am-5pm*).

Opposite the cathedral is Advocates Close and what is claimed to be the city's **oldest house** (no 8), built in 1450. It is a tall, narrow, picturesque building, currently occupied as a gallery and shop by DOM, an arts project featuring international artists working in Scotland. Their traditional and contemporary works sit well in this ancient setting.

Immediately past the cathedral stands the 19C **Mercat Cross** (market cross), part of which dates from the 16C. It is a traditional meeting point and in times past was the scene of demonstrations, executions and royal proclamations. Today it is a rendez-vous for

Mercat Tours, whose best known tour visits the underground street of **Mary King's Close** (*see* p.66).

The Royal Mile's second landmark church is the smoke-blackened **Tron Kirk**, taking its unusual name from a weighing machine (*tron* in old Scottish) which was once sited here. The building is closed at present.

The **Museum of Childhood** (*closed Sun*) was founded in 1955 by Patrick Murray, who curiously was a bachelor and professed not to like children. This marvellous collection, however, is a celebration of childhood and all the accoutrements and playthings that go with it. Think of a toy, doll, model or game from almost any era and the chances are that it will be here. Misty-eyed adults reminisce about

Crowds have gathered at the Mercat Cross over the ages to demonstrate, celebrate, cheer troops on their way to battle, to witness executions and hear royal proclamations.

Victorian dolls displayed at the Museum of Childhood.

long-forgotten toys while crackly black-and-white footage of old Edinburgh children's street games provide a glimpse of a vanished world.

Opposite the museum, on Chalmers Close, is another interesting visitor attraction that is more than mere child's play. The **Brass Rubbing Centre** (*closed Sun*) occupies Trinity Apse, the only surviving part of the Gothic Trinity College Church, founded around 1460 by Queen Mary, consort to James II. It was moved piece by piece from its original site, just down the hill, when Waverley Station was under construction, and rebuilt here.

Dating from around 1450, the John Knox House is a fine example of a mid-15C town house.

Back on the Mile, and almost as ancient, is the **John Knox House** (*closed Sun*). This much photographed property, the finest survivor of its period, was built in the mid 15C, though its present appearance is that of a 16C Edinburgh townhouse. Its somewhat tenuous association with Knox, who may have died here in 1572, saved it from demolition. It's well worth a visit to get a handle on Knox and the Reformation, a dry subject that is cleverly brought to life by contrasting the views of Knox with those of royalist goldsmith James Mossman (who owned the house) in an imaginary conversation. Even better is the transcript of the heated exchange that really did take place between Knox and Mary Queen of Scots, which is re-enacted on the top floor of the house. Knox's voice is suitably gruff and unyielding. Next door, the Netherbow Arts Centre marks the site of the old **Netherbow Port**, one of the city's original medieval gates. Here, old Edinburgh finished – hence the melodramatically named World's End pub opposite – and the burgh of Canongate began.

Canongate

The principal attractions of this less frequented end of the Royal Mile are its two historical museums. **The People's Story** (*closed Sun*) is a fascinating social history of the city, from the squalid conditions of the late 18C right up to the third Millennium. The organisation (and exploitation) of labour, living conditions, leisure pursuits and crime and punishment are some of its major themes. It is set in the old **Canongate Tollbooth★**, a late-16C building which in its time once functioned as a tax collection point, council chamber, police court and prison – a very apt home in which to document the hardships of ordinary Edinburgh folk. Don't miss the top-floor video

Providing a home for The People's Story museum is just the latest in a long line of uses the Canongate Tollbooth has been put to over the centuries.

of present-day Edinburgh citizens reminiscing about their own lives.

Almost opposite, also in a 16C building, Huntley House, is the **Museum of Edinburgh** (*closed Sun*). This is the foil for The People's Story – a more conventional museum featuring objects of significant historical value. Scale models of Old Edinburgh, reconstructed 17C and 18C rooms, a glittering collection of Edinburgh silver, pottery, the original copy of the fateful Covenant (*see* p.14), memorabilia of Greyfriars Bobby (*see* p.63) and a colourful collection of old shop signs are among its many items.

Canongate Church, low and curvilinear, built in 1688, is the antithesis of the soaring spires of the Tron and Tollbooth churches on the upper Mile. Its churchyard is of more interest than its interior, and holds the graves of economist Adam Smith (1723-90), who died next door in Panmure House, and the local poet Robert Fergusson (1750-74), the inspiration for Robert Burns, who paid for this present gravestone and composed its dedication. Burns' sweetheart, 'Clarinda' (real name Agnes McLehose) also lies here and a plaque on the east wall recalls her alias. To the right of the church is the (supposed) grave of David Rizzio (c.1533-1566), the murdered secretary of Mary Queen of Scots.

The Museum of Edinburgh is housed in the charming warren of rooms, corridors and narrow staircases of the 16C Huntley House.

EXPLORING EDINBURGH

Almost at the very bottom of the Mile is the most picturesque close of all. **White Horse Close** originally dated from the late 17C, which was completely remodelled in 1889 by the philanthropist Dr Barbour, to provide homes for low-paid workers; in 1962 it was again reconstructed to take on its present-day appearance.

Opposite is the ultra-modern complex known as the **Holyrood Building**, which will house the new Scottish Parliament. It is due to be completed in late 2002 and it is thought that members will take up their seats here around May 2003. Until then the **New Parliament Building Visitor Centre** on Holyrood Road (*closed Sun*) should answer most questions. (Note: as the opening date gets nearer, this visitor centre may be relocated for landscaping purposes.)

Just off the bustling Royal Mile are peaceful closes, such as White Horse Close, where you really feel you have stepped back in time.

THE NEW TOWN

In the mid 18C, as the Old Town tenements heaved under the strain of Edinburgh's ever-increasing population, the young architect James Craig won the competition to design the New Town (*see* p.15). The development of the marshy area north of the Old Town into the broad, elegant Georgian streets, arranged in a symmetrical grid pattern, interspersed with gardens, parks and linking splendid squares – a triumph of town planning – rapidly attracted the fashionable element of Edinburgh society. The contrast between Old and New Town could not have been greater, and such was the

The broad sweep of Princes Street boldly leads the way through the New Town.

success of the New Town that the original area – with the trio of George Street, Princes Street and Queens Street – was soon extended to the north, west and east with an extraordinary series of crescents, circuses, squares, parks and gardens.

Princes Street

While the Royal Mile is the historical centre of the city, and the Georgian splendour of the New Town starts a block north, Princes Street, for all its imperfections, is still the most photographed street in Edinburgh, and unmissable for its views and gardens.

Princes Street begins, for most visitors at

least, at **Waverley Station** and the main tourist information centre. From here, the skirl of the pipes can usually be heard, courtesy of a busking bagpiper. The grand palatial building next to the station is the **Balmoral Hotel**, a home-from-home for visiting presidents, dignitaries and rock stars. Built in 1902 (as the North British Station Hotel), its clock tower has become one of the city's most recognisable landmarks. The clock is always a couple of minutes fast so that travellers have a breathing space – a vestige of the days when watches were not so common!

The north side of Princes Street is mostly disappointing, devoted to a procession of

Calton Hill, Balmoral Hotel, North Bridge and Waverley Station, viewed from the Scott Monument.

bland, architecturally mismatched chain-stores. The main exception is **Jenner's** (*see* p.109). By contrast, the south side of the street is completely open, providing sweeping views across its beautiful gardens, including the most famous (though not the best) view of Edinburgh Castle. The beautifully-tended grassy **Princes Street Gardens** were created in the 1760s when the Nor'Loch – by that time less a loch (lake) than a vile cesspit – was drained. In summer, it's the perfect place for sitting and enjoying the view, admiring the statues, the famous summer floral clock (in the West Gardens) and letting the children run free.

The most famous structure in the Gardens,

The Scott Monument and Balmoral Hotel watch over the crowds enjoying the summer sun in Princes Street Gardens.

indeed in all Edinburgh, is the towering 61m (200ft) **Sir Walter Scott Monument★**. Designed in Gothic style by George Meikle Kemp and completed in 1846, it is frequently likened to a sky rocket. Scott and his faithful dog, Maida, sit below the pinnacled tower while 64 characters from Scott's novels appear in niches, along with the busts of 16 great Scottish poets. There are four viewing platforms spaced between the 287 steps, and the first floor has a small exhibition on Scott and the construction of the monument. The **views★** are good, if not spectacular, but anyone who is particularly large or claustrophobic would do well to avoid the extremely narrow dark steps at the very top.

Taking time to make a few adjustments to the Floral Clock in the gardens.

The Mound

The Mound joins Princes Street to the Old Town (via North Bank Street), and was originally built as a causeway over the marshy ground in between the two areas, from the late 18C to the 1830s, using an estimated 2 million cartloads of earth and rubble excavated during the construction of the New Town.

When the **Edinburgh Festival** is on, the Mound is buzzing with entertainers who use

this area as a place to advertise their show free of charge to crowds of delighted onlookers. In fact, buskers and street performers keep the Mound lively for most of the summer.

At any time of year, two national institutions make this a busy place for art lovers. The **Royal Scottish Academy**, whose Classical columns front onto Princes Street, is home to changing exhibitions, often of contemporary Scottish artists. Like its better known London cousin, it too has a Summer Exhibition, which any artist can enter. At present, the Academy is closed for refurbishment, which will include a new

The Scott Monument, one of Edinburgh's most famous landmarks, illuminated on a winter's night.

underground link to the National Gallery, a restaurant and additional educational and visitor facilities. It re-opens in 2003 with a major exhibition, *Monet at Vétheuil*.

The **National Gallery of Scotland★★**, housed in a similar Greek Revival building, is home to the national collections of European and Scottish art c.1300-1900. It features some outstanding European works and is one of Britain's best small to medium-sized galleries. You can easily explore it in a few hours without the feeling of sensory overload which larger galleries can induce.

The main floor is devoted mostly to 16C and 17C Italian, French, Spanish, Dutch and Flemish works. Look out for *The Virgin Adoring the Sleeping Christ Child* by Botticelli, the striking portrait of *The Ladies Waldegrave* by Reynolds, *Trinity Altarpiece* by Hugo Van der Goes, the four huge canvasses by Titian, Poussin's *Seven Sacraments*, Rembrandt's *Self Portrait Aged 51* and the dramatic *Murder of David Rizzio* by John Opie.

The National Gallery of Scotland and Edinburgh Castle, viewed from the Scott Monument.

The upper floor has a small but high quality collection of Impressionist paintings, with some instantly recognisable works by Monet (*Haystacks*), Degas (*Group of Dancers*), Gauguin (*Three Tahitians*), Van Gogh (*Les Oliviers/Olive Trees*), plus works by Cézanne and Seurat.

The Scottish Collection is dominated by portraiture. Nasmyth's *Edinburgh Castle and the Nor'Loch* and *The Porteous Mob* by Drummond (based on an historical riot in the Royal Mile) are of local interest, while most visitors' favourite work is Henry Raeburn's *The Reverend Robert Walker Skating on Duddingstone Loch*, a charming dreamy portrait which has become almost a city icon.

The gallery also stages top class touring exhibitions, and every January the outstanding Vaughan Bequest of J M W Turner Watercolours is on display for a month.

Do note that one of Britain's favourite sculptures, *The Three Graces* by Canova, owned jointly by the National Gallery of Scotland and the Victoria and Albert Museum, is at the V&A in London until 2006.

Impressionist paintings in the National Gallery of Scotland.

The Reverend Robert Walker Skating on Duddingstone Loch, *by Henry Raeburn, National Gallery of Scotland.*

For more art, of the modern kind, walk up the steps and turn left into Market Street to visit the **City Art Centre** and the **Fruitmarket** galleries. Also on Market Street is **The Edinburgh Dungeon**, featuring the darkest, goriest side of Edinburgh's history, including the vile deeds of Burke and Hare and the Leith cannibal, Sawney Beane, all portrayed in horrific life-like tableaux.

George Street

One block north of Princes Street, George Street, named after King George III, was planned as the spine of the New Town and is still the city's most elegant thoroughfare. In the last few years, it has once again become one of Edinburgh's most fashionable places, with a deliberate policy of encouraging high quality eating and shopping outlets.

At its eastern end it is bounded by St Andrew

Square, dominated by the **Melville Monument** referring to Viscount Melville, Henry Dundas (1724-1811). He was once the most powerful man in Scotland, and was nicknamed King Harry the Ninth. Many of the formerly private houses on and around this grand street are now banks, offices and shops, a prime example being **Dundas House★**, at no 36 St Andrew Square, now the headquarters of the Royal Bank of Scotland. It has a splendid entrance, though the domed banking hall was added later. An even more glorious domed banking hall can be enjoyed, drink in hand, further along George Street at no 14, in the recently converted pub, **The Dome**.

Other buildings along George Street which are open to the public and notable for their Regency interiors include the **Assembly Rooms**, now a popular concert venue, the Standing Order pub, and the George Intercontinental Hotel.

Originally built as a residence for Sir Lawrence Dundas, the magnificent Dundas House is now home of the Royal Bank of Scotland.

A frieze of famous figures from Scotland's past, painted by William Hole, circles the Great Hall balcony of the Scottish National Portrait Gallery.

Parallel to and north of George Street, on the eastern end of Queen Street, is the **Scottish National Portrait Gallery★**, which documents the country's most famous faces, past and present. It is housed in a remarkable Victorian neo-Gothic building, decorated on the outside with life-size sculptures and inside with a splendid glowing circular **frieze** around the Great Hall balcony, depicting 'famous' Scots, from the 19C historian Thomas Carlyle, back through Macbeth to Stone-Age man. Start on the top floor for the oldest pictures: Mary Queen of Scots, Bonnie Prince Charlie, Robert Burns, Sir Walter Scott and various (less) famous faces of lairds and notables, invariably clad in plaid. The first floor, which runs from Edwardian times to the present day, is the most fascinating. Exhibits rotate so you can never be too sure of what is on display, but among the highlights are David Mach's ingeniously composed dynamic large-scale portraits of current Scottish sporting stars which are interwoven with thousands of copies of the same postcard. The ground floor is devoted to temporary exhibitions, and has an excellent shop and café (*see* p.106).

Charlotte Square★★★

Bounding George Street to the west, **Charlotte Square★★★** is the city's finest Georgian ensemble, the work of the city's most eminent architect, Robert Adam, designed in 1791. A number of properties on the square are owned and cared for by the National Trust for Scotland, and three of these are open to the public.

At no 7, **The Georgian House★** has been refurbished as a typical home of the period from 1790 to 1810. Its kitchen is particularly

Charlotte Square – the epitome of Georgian elegance.

interesting. On the opposite side of the square, **Number 28** is even more attractive. Downstairs it houses one of the city's nicest tea rooms (*see* p.105) and a lovely gift shop, while upstairs is an exhibition of paintings by 20C Scottish artists. Next door at no 27 is a restaurant, serving top quality Scottish fare in an original Georgian dining room.

HOLYROOD AND CALTON HILL

Holyrood Abbey and Holyroodhouse Palace★★

The legend of Holyrood goes back some 900 years. While out hunting in 1128, the Scottish king, David I, was thrown from his horse and was about to be gored by an enraged stag. As he raised his hand to fend it off, his hand fastened on a gold crucifix in between the stag's antlers. The stag retreated; the crucifix turned out to be a piece of the True Cross (the Holy Rood) and in gratitude for his life being spared, the king founded **Holyrood Abbey**.

David's original Augustinian Abbey was replaced in 1190 by a much larger structure, which was sacked by Edward II in 1322 and later by Henry VIII. It continued to stage many royal events, including the Scottish coronation of Charles I in 1633. By the end of the 17C, however, the Abbey had fallen into disrepair, and misguided restoration only succeeded in bringing the roof down in 1768. Today it stands as a romantic ruin and may only be visited as part of the guided tour of Holyroodhouse Palace (*9.30am-4.30pm Nov-Mar, guided tours only; 9.30am-6pm Apr-Oct, visitors may tour freely. The Palace is also closed to visitors when the Queen and the Prince of Wales are here and for other events; for details* ☎ **0131 556 1096**).

Holyroodhouse Palace★★ began life as an Abbey guesthouse for the early kings, who are said to have preferred its comforts to that of the draughty castle a mile up the hill. The Stuart Kings, in particular, gave it great patronage: James II was born, married, crowned and buried here, and his three successors were also crowned at the Abbey. Around 1500, James IV had it built into a proper palace, though nothing remains of this structure and the earliest surviving part seen by today's visitors, the northern Tower (1528), is the work of James V. Severe damage was caused during the Reformation and by Cromwell's troops, and the palace which we see now is largely the work of Sir William Bruce, commissioned by Charles II in 1671. In more recent times, Holyroodhouse became a favourite of Queen Victoria when in Scotland, and the present queen, Elizabeth II, maintains the tradition of royal residence and hosts a garden party here each July.

Witness to royal births, marriages, deaths and even murder, Holyroodhouse Palace has long been a favourite residence of monarchs.

Visitors enter by The Great Stair, with its four 16C Brussels tapestries, which leads to the **State Apartments**, notable for their highly intricate decorative **plasterwork ceilings★★★**, lavishly carved woodwork and inset canvases.

The most curious room is the **Great Gallery**. In 1619, Jacob de Wet, whose work features throughout the palace, was commissioned to paint portraits of the 110 Scottish monarchs who had preceded his patron, Charles II. Having no historical reference for the vast majority of these, De Wet's solution – some say it was his instruction – was simply to make each into a Stuart look alike, with a protuberant nose as a defining characteristic. Look carefully at many of the faces and you will see they are virtually identical!

The Palace's most famous resident was **Mary Queen of Scots** (*see* p.12), who came to live here on her return from France in 1561. Here, four years later she married Lord Darnley, but by the time she was pregnant in 1566 (carrying the future James VI), their love had cooled. Mary sought solace and intellectual stimulation from her Italian secretary, David Rizzio, behaviour which enraged her jealous and volatile husband. In March 1566 Darnley and a group of his noblemen friends burst into Mary's chamber and stabbed Rizzio 56 times in front of the pregnant queen. She fled to Edinburgh Castle, where her son was born, but then returned to Holyroodhouse for another year or so until her imprisonment in Lochleven Castle.

The 'secret staircase' by which Darnley and his accomplices bypassed the Queen's guard is revealed; there is even a plaque and traditional 'bloodstain' which show where Rizzio fell. A splendid collection of objects associated with Mary and Darnley are displayed in the Outer Chamber – his armour, the magnificent

Darnley Jewel and many of Mary's personal items, including a fascinating segmented perfume pomander.

To celebrate Queen Elizabeth II's Golden Jubilee in autumn 2002, the former Holyrood Free Church and Duchess of Gordon's School at the Palace entrance will be opening as **The Queen's Gallery**, Edinburgh. This will stage changing exhibitions from the Queen's private collection, primarily drawing on the world-class drawings from the Print Room at Windsor Castle, including works by Michelangelo, Leonardo da Vinci, Raphael, Holbein, Claude and Canaletto.

Holyrood Park

This great green park is the largest area of open ground within the city and is dominated by two volcanic features: the highest point, an ancient volcanic plug, called Arthur's Seat, and the spiky ridge known as the Salisbury Crags.

The **Salisbury Crags** are the nearest, just ten minutes' walk from Holyroodhouse Palace; simply take any one of the paths leading straight up from Queen's Drive. The lower path which circles the hill, below the top of the Crags, is known as the Radical Road (built by labourers sacked from previous jobs because of their radical politics) but the views, looking down into the Old Town, are best from on the very top of the Crags.

There are numerous paths of varying degrees of difficulty leading to **Arthur's Seat**. From the Salisbury Crags, the easiest option is to walk to the right, anti-clockwise around the base of Arthur's Seat, and pick up the main road (Queen's Drive). Soon, down to your right, you will enjoy fine views of **Duddingston Loch**. Keep walking until you reach the car park at the much smaller Dunaspie Loch (around 30 minutes' walk in total). From here

On a bright, clear day, you can't beat climbing up to Arthur's Seat for its marvellous views and invigorating fresh air.

it is an easy 15-minute climb, straight across the road, to the top of Arthur's Seat. In good weather there are always local walkers to follow or to ask directions; in bad weather you probably won't want to come anyway, particularly if the chill east wind is blowing!

The summit may be only a modest elevation of 251m (823ft), but with its wonderful 360° **views**★★ you'll feel on top of the world: look south over the whole city, northwest to the Forth Bridges, north to Leith and northeast across the Forth to the Kingdom of Fife and beyond. Make your way back down to the Dunaspie Loch car park, follow the road back the way you came for a hundred metres or so, and turn off left down the steep grassy slope to pick up steps to the charming village of **Duddingston**. A plaque in the village marks the house on Causeway where it is thought that Bonnie Prince Charlie stayed in 1745, but it is the splendid Sheep's Heid pub (*see* p.103) which is the real reward for the weary walker.

Our Dynamic Earth, with the Salisbury Crags behind.

View from Calton Hill of the Dugald Stewart Monument, across the city to Edinburgh Castle.

Our Dynamic Earth

Occupying what appears to be a giant marquee, just below the dramatic Salisbury Crags, is Edinburgh's major Millennium visitor attraction, **Our Dynamic Earth**. This is an apt location for what is a truly dynamic and very dramatic exhibition on the natural and geological history of the earth, from its beginnings to the present day. This may sound an impossibly over ambitious brief, but right from the start, where you are transported into a glittering star chamber to 'witness' the Big Bang, it fairly gallops along, using just about every kind of modern tourist attraction stimulus to convince visitors they are riding aboard a glacier, hearing the crunch of dinosaurs' feet, being sprayed by a downpour in a rainforest, touching a real iceberg and so on. There are lots of clever state-of-the-art hands-on stations en route, and by the time you re-emerge into the 21C you really do feel that you have learned a lot more about the planet.

Calton Hill

If you haven't the time or energy to do Arthur's Seat or the Salisbury Crags, then Calton Hill, less elevated at 100m (328ft) but even more central, is the next best thing. If you have time for both, do both. The **views** from Calton Hill are among the best in the city centre and the motley collection of buildings, monuments and follies enhances its charm. Several of these are inspired by Greek architecture and were built during the late 18C when Edinburgh called itself 'The Athens of the North'.

The easiest approach to Calton Hill is from Waterloo Place, at the east end of Princes Street. From here, steps lead straight up to the 32m- (106ft-) tall **Nelson Monument** (*winter closes 3pm, closed Sun all year*). Built in 1807 as a monument to Admiral Lord Nelson, it

resembles an inverted telescope but, although this makes a nice maritime link, there is no evidence that it was intended. It is well worth climbing the 143 steps for a wonderful 360° **panorama★★★**, including the classic picture-postcard view along the length of Princes Street. Above your head a 'time ball', on the top of the flagpole, is hoisted up every day (*except Sunday*) and then dropped at 1pm precisely. It served as a visual signal to ships down below in the Firth of Forth and is a vestige of the days when maritime clocks were rare.

The Parthenon-like section of temple on top of the hill is known as the **National Monument**, and was begun in 1822 as a memorial to the dead of the Napoleonic Wars. It was intended to be a church that resembled the Parthenon but after a few years funds ran out and so the work stopped. The inability to complete it became a source of acute embarrassment – it became known as 'Scotland's Disgrace'

The incomplete National Monument (left) and Nelson Monument (right) – two of the more eccentric buildings on Calton Hill.

('Edinburgh's Disgrace' by Glaswegians!) and 'Edinburgh's Folly'. Come here late afternoon for great views down to Leith.

Another structure on the hill which takes its inspiration from Classical Greece is the elegant round colonnaded **Dugald Stewart Monument**, designed in 1831. Stewart was a professor of philosophy at the university, though the prominence and size of this memorial far outranks his historical importance, particularly when compared with the very similar and contemporary **Burns Monument** (dedicated to the national poet) close by.

The principal building on top of Calton Hill is the **Old City Observatory**, built 1776-1792 by James Craig and superseded by Playfair's building in 1818. By 1895, however, light pollution and smoke from the railway station below meant that it could no longer monitor the skies clearly so the observatory equipment was moved to new premises on Blackford Hill (in the southern suburbs), where it still resides today. The Astronomical Society opens the Old Observatory to the public every Friday evening for star gazing, but otherwise it is closed (☎ **0131 556 4365**). At the foot of the hill the **Royal High School** is another grand historic building (completed 1829), with a Greek Revival theme, also presently awaiting new occupants.

SOUTH OF THE ROYAL MILE

Greyfriars

Take the George IV Bridge off Lawnmarket, go past the ever-busy Elephant House café and you will come to a curious statue of a life-size Skye terrier, on a pedestal, outside the **Greyfriars Bobby** pub. The pub takes its name from the dog, who is the hero of Edinburgh's most heart-warming story, about which a Walt Disney film was made in 1961. His master, a policeman named John 'Jock' Gray, died in 1858 and was buried in Greyfriars churchyard (behind the pub). The ever-faithful Bobby, however, refused to leave his side and kept a constant vigil by his master's grave. The locals sheltered, fed and watered him and he remained here for 14 years, before being buried close by. His loyalty and devotion struck the people of Edinburgh so much that he became a city legend.

Loyal to the last, Bobby is remembered by this statue outside the Grey-friars Bobby pub.

Other legends associated with **Greyfriars Churchyard** are much less warming. It was here in 1638 that the National Covenant was signed, and also here that, in 1679, some 1 200 Covenanters were held prisoners in an unroofed compound in the south west corner of the churchyard for five months, throughout the winter. With no protection from the elements and minimal daily sustenance, many perished. Not surprisingly, tales of ghosts abound. The compound (marked Covenanters' Prison) is now locked and violent poltergeist activities have recently been reported. Yet even without such a grisly history, Greyfriars would still be the most atmospheric churchyard in Edinburgh. It is said that as many as 80 000 bodies lie here; its collection of ghoulish skull-and-bone adorned 17C **funeral monuments** is unparalleled. Their blackened, unkempt state only adds to the Hammer horror atmosphere, yet the outlook from the churchyard is also remarkably peaceful. With its many mature trees and surrounded by ancient buildings and

Stepping apprehensively into the darkness of the underground 'vaults', Mary King's Close, or the City of the Dead – senses straining, wondering if tonight there will be a sighting!

a part of the Flodden Wall, its almost bucolic appearance has changed little over the centuries. The spectacular 17C building next door is **George Heriot's School,** one of Scotland's finest. After the churchyard, the kirk itself, rebuilt in 1845, is quite ordinary, though worth a quick look if open at the time of your visit.

Royal Museum and Museum of Scotland★★★

Across the road and just along from Greyfriars, the **Museum of Scotland★★★** occupies a striking, critically-acclaimed, modern sandstone-faced building resembling a castle, opened in 1998 as an extension of the old Royal Museum. Its remit is the history of Scotland, from its geological formation and earliest peoples right through to the present day. It is a huge collection and too much to see in one visit. Its layout (due to change) is also difficult to navigate, so it is a good idea to take a Free Highlights guided tour (*tours daily 2.15pm, also 6pm on Tues. Both the Museum of Scotland and Royal Museum open Mon-Sat 10am-5pm, Sun noon-5pm, Tues until 8pm*). A sound guide which spotlights 50 favourite exhibits is also available. The museum is divided into sections each looking at key themes in the development of Scotland, arranged on seven levels.

  Beginnings (Lower Ground) is a fascinating look at how Scotland's land mass has evolved: from being near the South Pole some 650 million years ago, moving via the Equator, when it was hot and wet with coral reefs, to just north of the Equator, when it became mostly desert, through to its present position and cool northern clime. **Early People** covers prehistory from 8000BC-AD1100 and features some memorable statues by Eduardo Paolozzi showing off ancient jewellery.

The Haunted City

They say Edinburgh is one of the most haunted cities in Europe and anyone who has wandered the dim, steep, narrow wynds and closes of the Old Town after dark can see that this is fertile, classic ground for ghostly goings-on.

In medieval times, Edinburgh's dark, claustrophobic, insanitary conditions made it a truly terrible place in which to live. When plague visited – as it did frequently in medieval Europe – there was no escape. Drastic times called for drastic measures so, when in 1645 some of the inhabitants of Mary

King's Close (which runs beneath the present council chambers on the Royal Mile) caught the dreaded pox, it was decided that the whole street would be sealed off to stop the disease from spreading. Whether or not all the inhabitants were trapped inside, as happened in other city closes, is unclear but certainly many died down here. Not surprisingly, when Mary King's Close was eventually reopened, many apparitions were reported; recently psychics testing the veracity of the legend also attest to the strong presence of ghosts. Since 1997 Mercat Tours have been allowed to guide visitors through these labyrinthine passageways, and entertain and enthral with many a fascinating tale (Mercat Tours depart daily, bookings ☎ 0131 557 6464).

On the opposite side of the Mile, beneath South Bridge, lies more of Edinburgh's 'underground city' – closes and streets, hidden and forgotten, now generally referred to as 'the vaults'. Some of these are used by nightclubs, or as storage cellars, and

Left: Funeral monument in Greyfriars Churchyard.

many a haunting has been reported here, too. Mercat Tours will also take you inside these spooky caverns.

Edinburgh's most famous recent ghost does not dwell underground at all, but in the so-called City of the Dead, at Greyfriars Kirk, where in the 17C hundreds of Covenanter prisoners died in terrible conditions (*see* p.64). Yet it is not thought to be one of their souls which has recently started wandering but that of their chief prosecutor, James ('Bloody') McKenzie, ironically buried almost next door to their prison compound. In 1998 City of the Dead Tours (☎ **0131 447 2230**) were granted a licence to visit this area and during the last three years many attacks and incidents (scratches, bumps, bruising, intense cold and faintings) involving tour leaders and guests have been reported. It is now claimed that the McKenzie Poltergeist has become the best documented case of its kind in the last two centuries. Whatever the truth behind it, this tour, as the hype claims, really *is* the scary one.

EXPLORING EDINBURGH

The Kingdom of the Scots (Level 2) is a favourite with many visitors, covering the period 900-1707. Don't miss the 12C Lewis Chessmen, the Bute Mazer (a cup probably made for Robert the Bruce), the 'Maiden' (a Scottish guillotine) and Mary Queen of Scots' jewellery.

Scotland Transformed (1707-1914) (Level 3) looks at the Union with England and the Industrial Revolution, including a giant working Newcomen steam-driven engine. There are more large-scale engineering exhibits on the next floor's **Industry and Empire** (Levels 4/5), notably the 1861 steam locomotive *Ellesmere*, which had to be lowered into position before the levels above it were constructed. Finally, Scotland in the **Twentieth Century** (Level 6) is represented by some 300 objects selected by the Scottish public, from a television (chosen by the son of John Logie Baird) to an electric guitar (chosen by Prime Minister, Tony Blair) and, less glamorously, hypodermic syringes. The **Roof Garden**

The bold modern design of the Museum of Scotland provides a variety of stimulating settings in which its exhibits can be displayed.

(Level 7) offers splendid **views** across the castle and Royal Mile, the Pentland Hills and the Firth of Forth.

Adjacent to and linked to the Museum of Scotland, is the **Royal Museum**, a very different building. This handsome, classic, three-storey Victorian hall of plate glass and cast iron is home to Scotland's international collections of decorative arts, science, industry, archaeology and the natural world. It is eclectic in the extreme and offers a bewildering choice of exhibits, from Egyptian mummies to a Bubble Car, medieval armour to a 2.9m (9ft 6in) Japanese spider crab, Islamic art to pop memorabilia and the old Falkirk Town Clock. Among the many fascinating objects and galleries, look out for the following: main hall – *Wylam Dilly*, the world's oldest preserved locomotive (1813); ground floor – Natural Curiosity, Mammals, Art & Industry since 1850 and World in our Hands areas; first floor – Ancient Egypt, Western Decorative Art 1850-2000; on the second floor the Ivy Wu Gallery of Far Eastern Art is extremely beautiful. One item that is difficult to miss is the museum's marvellously macabre 10m-high **Millennium Clock Tower** (in the main hall). On each hour it gives a spectacular 5-minute mechanical performance. For the museum's choice of highlights take one of their free tours (*tours daily at 2.30pm; Sun 3.30pm*).

Grassmarket

The Grassmarket is one of Edinburgh's best known and oldest squares, with a market charter for livestock sales dating from 1477. The south side is modern, the north side almost wall-to-wall pubs, most of which attract the 18-25 age group, and in summer can be very boisterous. The punning Last Drop recalls that Grassmarket was an execution site; Robert

Burns is said to have taken inspiration while in The White Hart. The fine **view** up to the castle from the Grassmarket is much photographed.

Leading off Grassmarket, along the alleyway known as the Vennel, is a well preserved section of the **Flodden Wall**.

Grassmarket leads off southwest via West Port (the city's western gate) and East Fountainbridge, to Fountainbridge (bus nos 1, 28, 34, 35), where tucked inside the Fountainpark shopping and leisure complex you will find **Shaping A Nation**. It's an entertaining place, with plenty of interactive exhibits, focusing mostly on the many great people and inventions which Scotland has produced. It ends with an excellent vox pop film featuring ordinary Scots from all over the country, and a motion simulator ride across Scotland.

More than 100 Covenanters were hanged in the 17C Grassmarket, St Andrew's Cross in the cobblestones marking the site of the gallows.

CITY OUTSKIRTS AND VILLAGES

Dean Village and Stockbridge

Just a few minutes' walk from the city centre, to the northwest of the New Town, these two neighbouring villages have not only retained their distinct local identities but also host three of Edinburgh's favourite attractions: two outstanding galleries of modern art and Scotland's finest botanic gardens. As a bonus, you can walk from one to the other on the Water of Leith Walkway, a recently restored bucolic riverside path.

Start at the **Scottish National Gallery of Modern Art★**, on Belford Road. Set in a large 19C neo-Classical house in rolling parkland, this bright and cheery gallery is the sort of place that gives modern art a good name. It features works by Scottish artists and international luminaries including Andy Warhol, Roy Lichtenstein, Picasso and Matisse. British painters such as David Hockney, Stanley Spencer, Walter Sickert and L S Lowry are also well represented. Room 7, devoted to Pop Art, is a favourite with most visitors, complete with two famous life-size '*Tourists*'. If the room is busy, you may not even spot them until you bump into them. The Edinburgh School and Scottish Colourists are well represented in the comprehensive Scottish Collection.

Across the road, the **Dean Gallery★** is also home to some very accessible modern art, and leans heavily on the works of Edinburgh-born Eduardo Paolozzi, famous for his trademark 'man-machine' sculptures. His giant two-storey *Vulcan* is a classic, and there is a fascinating re-creation of his studio. The Dean Gallery is also very strong on Dada and Surrealism, with some remarkable works by Dali, Magritte, Miró, Duchamp, Ernst and Tanguy. Both galleries have excellent cafés and first-class shops.

The **Water of Leith Walkway** flows right below the Gallery of Modern Art – just follow the signs in the grounds. Turn left onto the path and after about 5-10 minutes you will pass through picturesque **Dean Village**, set to either side of a deep gorge. The river once powered 11 mills here and relics still remain. After another 5-10 minutes you will arrive in **Stockbridge**, a good place for lunch, with some excellent restaurants. Continue along the walkway for another five minutes until you reach the bend of Glenogle Road and St Stephenson's Row, where you leave the Walkway. Turn left, then immediately right into Arboretum Avenue and follow the road around. Across the Water of Leith, to your right, the picturesque row of dwellings are part of the housing project known as **The Colonies**, built for local workers in the 1860s.

Vulcan, *by Eduardo Paolozzi, in the Dean Gallery.*

Continue along Inverleith Terrace Lane and right into Inverleith Row. A short distance along on the left is the entrance to the **Royal Botanic Garden★★★**. Edinburgh's original Royal Botanic Garden was established in 1670, next to Holyroodhouse Palace, as a physic garden for early medical research purposes. It moved to its present 28ha (72 acre) site in 1823 and has been popular with locals and visitors ever since. Despite the serious research which still goes on here, this is a great place to simply wander, or for children to run around in, with large grassy areas and an arboretum with many well-established trees. In spring, don't miss the brilliant colours of the Rhododendron Walk.

The highlight throughout the year is **The Glasshouse Experience**, a complex of ten linked glasshouses, including the Palm House, Britain's tallest at 21m (70ft). Here you can pass through tropical, temperate and arid climes, spotting exotic orchids, lush tall palms, delicate cycads and ferns, desert plants and (in summer) giant water lily-pads.

Leith

The Water of Leith eventually runs into the Firth of Forth at Leith, Edinburgh's port since the 14C. In the second half of the 20C, with the decline of big ships and heavy industry, it slumped into inner-city dereliction and acquired a very bad reputation (the tale of low-life drug addicts in the 1991 film *Trainspotting* originated here). Since the mid 1980s, however, it has been revitalised into a trendy docklands development area, with advertising agencies and the new Scottish Office building

Escape from the city bustle (and the weather!) in the Royal Botanic Garden.

providing well-paid jobs. Loft homes have been created in old dockside warehouses, old boozers have been gentrified and a rash of style bars, gourmet restaurants and night-clubs have sprung up. Go down to The Shore area and check it out.

Another welcome Leith newcomer is the **Royal Yacht *Britannia*★** which, after 44 years, one million miles, 600 ports and 135 countries, was decommissioned in 1997 and is now permanently moored here as a floating museum (shuttle buses operate between Waverley Bridge and *Britannia*, run by Guide Friday and LRT). Whether you are royalist or republican this is a fascinating visit, with an excellent introductory exhibition which tells you everything you ever wanted to know about

Just a few dinner guests expected, on the Royal Yacht Britannia.

Close encounters with a Jaguar, at Edinburgh Zoo.

the royals afloat (it is advisable to pre-book in August, ☎ **0131 555 5566**). Once aboard, visitors follow a set trail, with an entertaining audio guide which takes you from engine room to royal apartments and bedrooms, and with refreshing candour sheds light on such frivolous crew pastimes as 'wombat tennis' (played with a soft toy!). Directly opposite *Britannia*, the new **Ocean Terminal** by Terence Conran is Leith's latest temple to conspicuous consumption and hopes to attract cruise ships to the city.

Edinburgh Zoo★★

About 3km (2 miles) west of the city, set on a steep hill on the main road to the airport (bus nos 12, 26, 31), **Edinburgh Zoo★★** enjoys a lovely setting. It is one of Britain's finest zoological parks, achieving great success in its breeding programmes and endangered species conservation projects. Most of the family favourites are here and the zoo is famous for its penguin colony, the largest in captivity (don't miss the daily Penguin Parade if it's on). It's quite a climb to the top of Corstorphine Hill but worth it to see the big cats collection and (quite separate) 'The African Plains' with zebra, ostrich and antelope (*open daily 9am-6pm Apr-Sept; daily 9am-4.30pm Oct-Mar*).

Rosslyn Chapel★★

Rosslyn Chapel★★, 10km (6 miles) south of the city centre, boasts the finest example of medieval stone carving in Scotland, if not Britain. It was built in 1446 by Sir William St Clair, third and last Prince of Orkney, and is steeped in legend, with much pagan symbolism (look out for the recurring Green Man), freemason connections and a whole host of mysteries. Most famous is the carving of Indian Corn (sweetcorn), found only in the New World, made 100 years before Colombus. Could it have been brought back by Henry St Clair, first Prince of Orkney, the 'true discoverer' of America? The finest carving of all is on the fantastically twisted **Apprentice Pillar★★★**. It is said to have been carved by an apprentice in his master's absence. When the master returned, he killed the boy in a fit of jealousy.

The Apprentice Pillar, in Rosslyn Chapel.

EXCURSIONS

The following day trips are all within a maximum 60 minutes' drive of Edinburgh. Most are well served by public transport, though if you want to visit Culross and the historic properties around South Queensferry you will need your own transport. Organised coach tours visit both Stirling and the Borders.

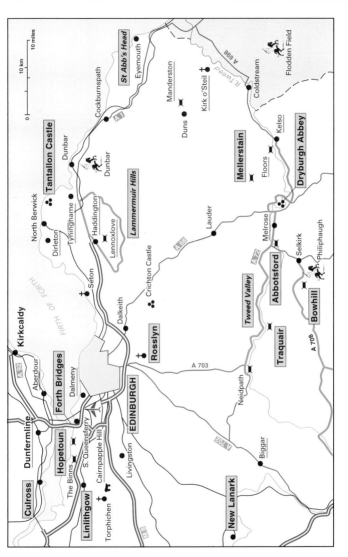

SOUTH QUEENSFERRY

The first regular ferry service at South Queensferry was established about 1129, to take pilgrims across the Forth to visit the shrine of St Andrew (at the present-day St Andrews), but well before that Queen Margaret (1046-93), consort of Malcolm III, used to cross here on her frequent journeys between Edinburgh and the royal palace at Dunfermline, and so gave Queensferry its name. These days, it is famous for its spectacular modern river crossings, the **Forth Bridges★★**.

By the time the famous **Forth Rail Bridge** was completed in 1890, it had taken 54 000 tons of steel, 6.5 million rivets and, in the course of seven years, cost the lives of 57 men to build. It was hailed as 'The Eighth Wonder of the World' and at the time was the biggest bridge on earth. Its statistics are still impressive today: its familiar cantilever arches reach a height of 111m (365ft) above the water; a tube train could drive through its 4m (12ft) diameter columns; it takes four years and 32 000 litres (7 000 galls) to repaint; a shower of rain adds around 100 tons and in hot weather it expands

The Forth Rail Bridge and Forth Road Bridge span the Firth of Forth in grand style.

up to 2m (7ft). At night it is spectacularly floodlit.

Almost as impressive is the adjacent **Forth Road Bridge**, opened in 1964 and also a world-record breaker in its day as the longest suspension bridge (2.4km/1.5 miles). The main towers of this elegant suspension bridge are almost half as tall again as the Rail Bridge, at 155m (512ft). The Road Bridge is also open to pedestrians and the **views** are magnificent. For more information on both bridges, visit the local **Queensferry Museum** or the **Forth Bridges Visitor Centre**, at the Queensferry Lodge Hotel on the north side of the road bridge.

In summer, the *Maid of the Forth* sails downstream from under the Rail Bridge, with guided commentary, to **Inchcolm Island**, where a picturesque ruined 15C abbey, seal spotting (sightings are virtually guaranteed) and birdwatching opportunities await.

More wildlife is to be seen just across the Forth Road Bridge at the entertaining **Deep Sea World**, a new state-of-the-art aquarium featuring the world's longest underwater tunnel (112m/367ft) allowing rays and sharks to pass safely within a few inches of your head.

HISTORICAL HOUSES

Within a 5-minute drive of South Queensferry are three stately homes, and just a little further afield is the ruined royal palace of Linlithgow. **Dalmeny House★** (*open Sun-Tue, July-Aug*) was built in 1815 in Gothic Revival style, for the Earl of Rosenberg. The superb furnishings include many items originating from the Rothschild collection from the Mentmore Estate.

The House of the Binns (*open Sat-Thur, May-Sept*), home of the Dalyell family, is set on a hilltop overlooking the Firth of Forth. The

house dates from the 17C and has some fine plasterwork **ceilings★**, as well as an interesting collection of momentoes of the family hero, General Tom, a staunch Royalist. At the execution of Charles I he swore never to cut his beard or hair until the monarchy was restored. He was imprisoned in the Tower of London and later served under the Czar of Russia but he returned to Scotland to lead the king's army under Charles II.

Often described as Scotland's finest stately home, **Hopetoun House★★** (*open daily, Mar-Sept; weekends only, Oct*) is a pompous 18C pile showcasing the talents of Scottish architects Sir William Bruce and William Adam. Its 40ha (100 acre) grounds include a Red Deer Park and Spring Garden with a profusion of wild flowers. Bruce's mature Classical influence can still be seen in the basic square structure and on the western façade. In 1721 William Adam was commissioned to extend the house. His eastern front engulfed the original house, with

Pine wainscotting and paintings by William McLaren decorate Bruce's sombre staircase at Hopetoun House.

magnificent curved colonnades, flanked on either side by projecting pavilions. His style continues in the lavish state apartments – especially the Red and Yellow Drawing Rooms – which also house a notable collection of furniture, paintings and tapestries.

Linlithgow Palace★★ is famous for its connections with Mary Queen of Scots and was also the last residence of her husband, Lord Darnley, before his murder in 1567. It was made into a royal palace by James I in 1435 and Mary Queen of Scots was born here in 1542. When, however, her son became James I of England in 1603 and moved the court to London, it fell into disuse and disrepair. In 1746 it burned down to its present state, a picturesque roofless shell. Despite its lack of a roof, you can still explore the maze of rooms, climb the spiral staircases and imagine the original magnificence of the huge Great Hall, which runs the whole length of the east side, or the sumptuous feasts that were prepared in the vast fireplace in the kitchen. Climb up to the

Linlithgow Palace's once glorious past is still evident from the evocative ruins that remain today.

The old and the new meld together at St Michael's Church, Linlithgow Palace.

top for fine **views** across the adjacent loch and surrounding countryside. Next to the palace, **St Michael's★**, famous for its recently added crown-of-thorns aluminium spire, is considered one of Scotland's finest medieval churches.

DUNFERMLINE★

Today the ancient seat of Scottish kings, **Dunfermline★**, is an attractive, relaxing little town which can easily keep you occupied for a day. About a thousand years ago it became the stronghold of Malcom Canmore (King Malcolm III), who married the saintly Queen Margaret. She introduced the Benedictine Order to Scotland and her son, King David I, built a great Benedictine Abbey here in 1250.

Margaret was canonised and Dunfermline became one of medieval Europe's great pilgrimage centres.

The best place to start is at the pink-painted **Abbot House**, the oldest dwelling in town, dating from the 15C. It was the administrative headquarters of the Benedictine Abbey and today is an award-winning museum and heritage centre, with some fascinating interiors and historic exhibits which touch upon virtually every aspect of life in Dunfermline over the last millennium.

Dunfermline Abbey★ consists of two churches: the giant atmospheric empty nave of the **Abbey Church★★**, built by David I and representing one of the finest Norman naves in

Scottish hero Robert the Bruce is remembered on the tower of the Parish Church at the east end of Dunfermline Abbey.

Scotland, and the modern **Parish Church** at the
east end, dedicated in 1821 (*open daily, Apr-Sep;
closed Fri/Sun mornings, Thur afternoon Oct-Mar*).
A gleaming brass plaque marks the resting
place of Scotland's most famous king, Robert
the Bruce, and his name is spelled out in large
stone letters around the spire. In the
churchyard is the grave of the mother of
William Wallace, Scotland's other immortalised
freedom fighter.

South of the Abbey Church is an assemblage
of ruined walls which once comprised the
monastic buildings – a refectory with chambers
below, the gatehouse and kitchen. Adjacent are
the ruins of Malcolm III's **Royal Palace**. It was
used by Scottish royalty until 1603 when the
court moved to London. Charles I, who was
born here, was the last monarch to visit, and
thereafter it fell into disrepair.

Dunfermline's most famous son is **Andrew
Carnegie**, born in 1835, a stone's throw from
the Abbey. He emigrated to the United States
in 1848 and made his fortune in the steel
industry. He became the world's richest man
and the greatest philanthropist of his time,
donating generously to his home town. His
birthplace is now a museum (*open daily,
Apr-Oct*).

CULROSS ★★

Now a quiet and very picturesque backwater,
Culross★★ (pronounced *Koo-ross*) is regarded as
the finest and most complete example of a
17-18C Scottish town, even though in today's
terms it is a mere village. Coal mining, which
made the town famous, was started by the
monks of **Culross Abbey** in the 13C and
reached its zenith with the remarkable
underwater mine of local magnate George
Bruce in the late 16C-early 17C. Culross
became a thriving port and contributed so

The Town House, at the heart of the pretty village of Culross, houses a museum about this quaint backwater.

much to the coffers of King James VI that he visited here in 1617 and bestowed upon the town the title of Royal Burgh. **Culross Palace★★**, built between 1597 and 1611 for Bruce, is named in honour of his visit, though the king never actually stayed here and the building is not, in the modern sense, at all palatial. It is, none the less, a remarkable and unique example of a restored merchant's house from this period and well worth a visit. Like much of Culross, it is administered by the National Trust for Scotland, who also look after the neighbouring **Bishop Leighton's Study★** and **Town House** (*all open daily, Apr-Sept; weekends only Oct*). In the latter, you can learn more about the history of Culross and how the Industrial Revolution passed it by, thus helping to preserve the ancient appearance of this delightful **village★★★**.

STIRLING★★

In medieval times **Stirling★★**, the natural gateway to the Highlands, was the key to Scotland, owing to its strategic position at the head of the Firth of Forth. Towering above all was (and still is) its dramatically sited castle. Today's structure dates mostly from the 15C and 16C, though the hill upon which it sits was probably occupied a millennium or so before then. **Stirling Castle★★** is closely associated with Mary Queen of Scots who was crowned here, and the Great Hall (recently restored) and Royal Palace Apartments (in the process of restoration) recall memories of her. Most impressive is the French-influenced **exterior★★★** of the **Palace** and the marvellous views from the summit.

Stirling Castle looks out over two of the most important battlefields in Scottish history – Stirling Bridge (1297) and Bannockburn (1314). Close to the site of the former is the **National Wallace Monument★★**, a magnificent

Climb the National Wallace Monument for stunning views over Stirling.

Stirling Castle, the gateway to the Highlands, is dramatically situated high on a crag overlooking the Forth river plains.

stone tower 67m (220ft) tall, built in 1868 to honour the Scottish victor of the battle, William Wallace. A patriotic exhibition inside the tower tells the story of Wallace, and the wonderful **views**★★ from the top outstrip even those from the castle.

More prosaic, though no less interesting, is the story of the Battle of Bannockburn, well told at the **Bannockburn Heritage Centre** 3km (2 miles) south of the castle. The battle was won by Wallace's freedom-fighting successor, King Robert the Bruce, whose mighty **equestrian statue** on part of the actual battlefield should not be missed.

THE BORDERS

The appeal of the Scottish Borders lies in the gentle rolling pastoral countryside, the romantic ruined abbeys and Walter Scott connections. An enjoyable circuit can be made from Edinburgh following the A68 via **Thirlestane Castle** (*open Sun-Fri, Easter-Oct*), to Earlston. Here, take the B6356 to **Scott's View**★★, a wonderful viewpoint made famous by Sir Walter Scott, whose **Abbotsford** home (*open daily, Apr-Oct*) is just a few miles west, beyond Melrose. There are picturesque abbey ruins in **Melrose**★★ where the heart of Robert the Bruce is reputed to lie (*open daily, all year*), nearby at **Dryburgh**★★ where Scott is buried (*open daily, all year*) and, perhaps finest of all, 16km (10 miles) east at **Kelso**. Kelso is also home to Scotland's largest inhabited castle, **Floors** (*open daily, Easter-Oct*).

Either take the A7 back to Edinburgh via Galashiels or make a detour 19km (12 miles) east to Scotland's oldest inhabited house, **Traquair**★★, near Innerleithen, which dates from 1107, and was visited by Mary Queen of Scots in 1566 (*open daily, late Apr-Oct; afternoons only Easter-May and Sept-Oct*).

SPIRIT OF EDINBURGH

Edinburgh is a dramatic city in almost every sense, and the best way to start to appreciate this is to arrive by train on a bright summer morning, at Waverley Station. There's no lift up to ground level, only many steps, but – as you will soon discover – Edinburgh's topography has more ups and downs than the Loch Ness monster, so perhaps it's best to get into training as soon as you arrive. The sight that greets you as you emerge blinking into the daylight is like no high street anywhere in the world. Turn to your left and you will see a great black stone skyrocket – the Scott Monument – often with a busking bagpiper beside it. Behind are gardens so green that it looks as if someone has painted the grass the night before. This bucolic stretch runs for almost 500m east-west, dipping steeply north-south

into a hollow where a loch once was, before rising up again to meet the Old Town. On the very top, on a brooding inaccessible crag, lording it over the city, is the famous castle.

Walk past the skyrocket, and the skirl of the pipes, to the Mound, a broad causeway that winds yellow-brick-road fashion up to the Old Town. Beside it, next to the Greek-Revival columns of the National Gallery

of Scotland, a man is sitting on a tall unicycle, juggling burning torches, joking with his audience and pretending to career out of control towards them. At Festival time he'll be joined by 'alternative' magicians and comedians, African acrobats, perhaps a performance of Macbeth to an audience of one in a motorcycle sidecar. Welcome to Edinburgh!

Like two other famously friendly north European capitals, Dublin and Amsterdam, what helps make Edinburgh so enjoyable is its compact size. You can walk from one end of the city centre to the other in half an hour, and across its breadth in less than an hour. Yet within that small area there are world-class museums and galleries, a great castle, an ancient palace still occasionally inhabited by royalty, stunning Georgian architecture, great individual shops and restaurants and, of course, a pub or two.

If you want to get into the spirit of Edinburgh before you arrive, then the written page is the best bet. For classic fiction try *The Prime of Miss Jean Brodie* by Muriel Spark; for a contemporary view get hold of one of Iain Banks' many Detective Rebus novels.

Surprisingly for the city that gave the world *Dr Jekyll and Mr Hyde*, Sir Walter Scott's *Waverley*

Edinburgh Castle and Princes Street Gardens at Christmas.

Busy shoppers in Lawnmarket.

novels and latterly Irvine Welsh's infamous *Trainspotting*, Edinburgh on film is something of a rarity. Look out for *Mary Reilly*, with John Malkovitch (a twist on the Jekyll and Hyde theme), and *Shallow Grave*, from the *Four Weddings and a Funeral/Notting Hill* team.

WEATHER

The only weak link in this great city's armour. There *are* sunny days, though the mercury rarely rises above 18°C in high summer; the best months are usually May and June. In winter, particularly when the east wind blows, temperatures plummet to the wee small numbers. Although Edinburgh is on the drier east coast of Scotland, it can, and frequently does, rain at any time of year, and proximity to the coast and hills means that the weather is changeable throughout the day, so don't be misled by a bright start. Warm summer days can also be blanketed by the local sea mist, the *haar*, which envelops the city. In short, expect the worst – you may be pleasantly surprised!

CALENDAR OF EVENTS

25 January *Burns Night* Haggis, neeps, tatties and whisky are consumed in pubs and restaurants, while a piper plays and the poems of Burns are puzzled over by confused visitors on the Bard of Scotland's birthday.

April *Edinburgh International Science Festival* Events and lectures on a wide range of subjects are held throughout the city, with lots of hands-on events for the children.

April 30 *Beltane* This ancient ritual of seasonal rebirth was reborn on Calton Hill in 1988 and has been going strong ever since, with lots of drumming, fires and dressing up. The starring roles go to the May Queen and the Green Man.

May *Scottish International Children's Festival* The turn of the youngsters to enjoy Edinburgh's propensity for a good festival, with performing arts, magic, mime and puppet shows.

Third week in June *Royal Highland Show* The highlight of Scotland's country calendar, featuring all things rural – food, livestock, flowers, crafts and more.

Last week in July, first week in August *Jazz and Blues Festival* First class j 'n' b percolates from the city's smokiest dives to its smartest theatres, out into the fresh air of Princes Street Gardens, and also Grassmarket, where a mini Carnival takes place.

August *Edinburgh Festival* The mainstream International Festival, the Military Tattoo and The Fringe last for three weeks, the Film Festival and the Book Festival last two weeks (*see* p.95). A fantastic Firework Concert takes place in Princes Street Gardens

on the last Saturday of the Festival.
September *Open Doors Day* Take a
look behind closed doors as some
of the finest historical and architecturally interesting private
houses and buildings in
Edinburgh are opened to the
public (usually over a weekend at
the end of the month).

29 December-2 January
Hogmanay The Scots take New
Year's Eve (Hogmanay) seriously
– in fact, it's now Europe's biggest
winter festival and is spread over
five days to dilute its excesses. It
includes street parties, fireworks
and processions with firebrands;
the burning of a Viking-style

longboat is a recent addition.
Beware that some pubs close early
on New Year's Eve so that publi-
cans can celebrate at their own
private parties. Also, because of
the crush in the city centre, you
are not allowed into the most
central area without a ticket (free
but you must obtain it in advance).

*The noise, sound, colour and
atmosphere of the Edinburgh
Tattoo, orchestrated to perfection
against the floodlit castle
and the twinkling
city lights below.*

The Edinburgh Festival

For decades now, Edinburgh and the word 'festival' have become almost synonymous. The **Edinburgh International Festival** started in 1947 and, by the end of the 1950s its off-spring, the **Edinburgh Festival Fringe**, had established its own niche. Today, it is the biggest and best arts festival in the world. In 2000 over 1 000 companies from 36 countries packed over 1 500 shows into 200 venues in 23 days.

The more formal mainstream International Festival lasts three weeks and comprises over 150 performances of world-class opera, dance, theatre and classical music, staged in the city's finest concert halls. Meanwhile, nightly on the Castle Esplanade, the **Edinburgh Tattoo** is the army's show and parade. It is watched live by 200 000 people over the period and is televised to millions more. The Fringe has an anarchic tabloid-led image; to the casual onlooker it may well seem that the main goal is to upstage the previous year's events by doing something even more extreme or more sensational than before. Juggling chain saws and body piercing with 6-inch nails, for

example. Being banned, it seems, is the ultimate accolade! Fringe performances crop up literally anywhere and everywhere; the 'troupe' who in 1979 performed *2001 – A Space Odyssey* in the front of a small car to an audience of two in the back, no doubt thought that was unbeatable – until someone did Shakespeare in a motorcycle and sidecar.

Despite these excesses, the simple truth is that the majority of Fringe events are well-staged serious works, with many going on to great mainstream success. True to the Fringe's original spirit, most acts are usually irreverent (but rarely too offensive) and many are enormous fun. In fact, anyone who enjoys the performing arts, in whatever guise, should beat a path to the city in August. You will need to book well ahead for the International Festival and big-name acts on the Fringe but for the rest of the Fringe the best policy is often to wait and see. Go to the Mound where you can enjoy free preview performances or pick up the local papers which give away a limited number of tickets to the first readers who can collect them; do read the previous night's reviews; good word-of-mouth can stimulate ticket sales like wildfire.

It may be hard to imagine but, while all this is going on, in Charlotte Square Gardens the **Edinburgh Book Festival** is staging the biggest public book event in the world, and at the city cinemas the **Film Festival** is in full swing.

For more details of all the above, click on the following web sites:
www.eif.co.uk
(for the International Festival)
www.edintattoo.co.uk
www.edfringe.com
www.edfilmfest.org.uk
www.edbookfest.co.uk

Call in at the Festival Fringe Society, High Street, Royal Mile.

ACCOMMODATION

As befits its capital status, Edinburgh has a good stock of four-star and five-star **hotels**, with more under construction to accommodate the delegates and associates of the new Parliament.

The overall standard of accommodation in Edinburgh is also good. Hotels tend to be individual and characterful as opposed to boxy Transatlantic chain-style and, unlike London, need not break the bank. There are a small number of high quality serviced **apartments** – expect to pay four-star hotel prices.

August – Festival time – is when rates for beds increase and availability is at a premium, but a recent influx of cheaper chain-hotel places means that there is usually space to be found somewhere.

If you are looking for something cheaper than a hotel, the city is well stocked with friendly **bed and breakfast** and **guest house** accommodation.

For the truly impecunious, the good news is that Edinburgh is well accustomed to backpackers' budgets and ridiculously cheap accommodation can be found in three **hostels** on or just off the Royal Mile. Rooms in university halls out of term time is another attractive option, ☎ **0131 651 2007**.

The Edinburgh & Lothians Tourist Board provides a booking

service for most types of accommodation, at any of its offices. The main one is south of Waverley Station, at 3 Princes Street ☎ **0131 473 3800**, www.edinburgh.org. There is a small non-refundable booking fee for this service.

The following prices are a guide to what you can expect to pay for a double room in a central hotel per night per person, usually with breakfast (but do check first). However, special off-peak rates, standby deals and other offers may dramatically reduce these prices. A number of hotels offer significant reductions on short breaks between October and March.

5-Star hotel £80-100
4-Star hotel £60-80
3-Star hotel £40-60
2-Star hotel £25-40

The Michelin *Red Guide Great Britain and Ireland* lists accommodation and restaurants in Edinburgh and the surrounding area, and is updated annually.

Recommendations

Expensive

The Balmoral *1 Princes Street, EH2 2EQ* ☎ **0131 556 2414** Fax 0131 557 3747. If it's good enough for President Clinton, Madonna and The Rolling Stones, then it's good enough for anyone. Ask for a room on the south or the east side for marvellous views. A swimming pool is among its many comforts.

George Intercontinental *19-21 George Street, EH2 2PB* ☎ **0131 225 1251** Fax 0131 226 5644. Beautifully appointed classic New Town hotel, with original Georgian interiors, including its famous cupola-covered breakfast area restaurant. Ask for a rear-facing room for great views over the Firth of Forth.

Crowne Plaza *80 High Street, Royal Mile, EH1 1TH* ☎ **0131 557 9797** Fax 0131 557 9789. Very comfortable and quiet, modern international-class hotel on the upper part of the Royal Mile, cleverly disguised as a sandstone-faced Scots baronial tower house. Small pool.

Moderate

Edinburgh First *Holyrood Park Road* ☎ **0800 287 118**. Unbeatable location and great value in an attractive modern block of University rooms in Holyrood Park. Only available Mar-Apr, Jun-Sept.

Best Western Bruntsfield *69 Bruntsfield Place* ☎ **0131 229 1393**. Quiet, comfortable, stylish four-star Victorian townhouse hotel, with good pub attached (no noise). Characterful local shops adjacent, and nice views over Bruntsfield Links parkland. Ten minutes' walk from the centre.

Best Western Braid Hills *134 Braid Road* ☎ **0131 447 8888**. This handsome four-star Scots Baronial pile is slightly south of the centre (10-15 minutes by bus)

The Balmoral hotel.

but enjoys an elevated position with views to the Castle and even to the Firth of Forth. Smart large rooms, some with great views. A good choice for touring and golfing.

The Bank *1 South Bridge, Royal Mile* ☎ **0131 556 9940** Fax 0131 558 1362. Set in a former bank building at a noisy intersection of the Royal Mile, this individualistic hotel offers nine rooms, each themed to a famous Scot with lots of matching paraphernalia. Lively bar downstairs so not for the early-to-beds.

Moderate/Inexpensive

Apex International Hotel *31-35 Grassmarket* ☎ **0131 300 3456** Fax 0131 220 5345. This modern, stylish three-star hotel is situated in the lively Grassmarket, with great views of the castle from its restaurant and many of the bedrooms. Some rooms have two double beds, so halving the cost for a family of four.

Inexpensive

Ailsa Craig *24 Royal Terrace, EH7 5AH* ☎ **0131 556 1022** Fax 0131 556 6055. The large Georgian rooms of this three-star hotel offer very good value (particularly if an extra bed is added). It also enjoys a nice location in a quiet residential area just below leafy Calton Hill, with views from some rooms to the Forth.

FOOD AND DRINK

With its huge, unspoiled tracts of rich pasture land, its many lochs and hundreds of miles of coastline, the traditional food of Scotland is based on beef (Aberdeen Angus is king), lamb, game (pheasant, partridge, grouse and venison), fish and shellfish (salmon, trout and lobster), soft fruits (raspberries and gooseberries) and winter vegetables.

Despite all this, it is a sad fact that the native diet is one of the unhealthiest in the world. Many unreconstructed Scotsmen still boast that they never eat vegetables or fruit, and even on the Royal Mile is a sign 'We sell Mars Bars in batter'. Thankfully, this is not typical of Edinburgh's culinary mainstream.

Breakfast

If you really want to go native, start the day with **porridge** – sprinkle it with salt, not sugar! After that, a full cooked breakfast with black pudding (pig's blood sausage), white pudding (a vegetarian version of black pudding) or perhaps haggis should be a doddle. A lighter Scottish choice is **kippers** (smoked herring) – the Loch Fyne variety are famous; or **Finnan Haddie** (haddock smoked over peat), perfect with a poached egg on top. An **Arbroath Smokie** is a haddock smoked over birch or oak twigs.

Typically Scottish

Haggis is the unofficial national dish, most apparent on Burns Night and, to a lesser degree, on St Andrew's Day (30 November) and at Hogmanay (New Year). If you intend to try it, it's probably best not to know what goes into it: the chopped-up heart, liver and lights (lungs) of a sheep, cooked with oatmeal and onions inside its stomach bag. Strange to say, it tastes quite good; even stranger, the vegetarian version – which seems like a contradiction in terms – is also worth a try. Haggis is traditionally accompanied by 'bashed (mashed) **neeps**' (confusingly, swede to the English, turnips to the Scots) and '**chappit tatties**' (mashed potatoes). Mashed tatties and neeps are also collectively known as **clapshot**. A wee dram of whisky helps it all down nicely. Haggis is on sale in many shops and as bar food in some Edinburgh pubs all year round. You will also find in pubs and cheaper cafés a dish called **stovies**, comprising sliced potatoes cooked in fat with onions and lamb (or perhaps minced beef) and maybe cabbage.

In the bakers, you will see **mutton pies** (also known as Scotch pies), small and round, made from hot-water pastry and filled with mutton. **Bridies**, also known as Forfar Bridies, are a sort of flaky Scottish puff pastry envelope filled with minced beef, vegetables and onion.

Traditional Scottish **soups** include cock-a-leekie (chicken and leek), cullen skink (fish and potato), Scotch broth (mutton or beef stock, vegetables and pearl barley) and partan bree (a creamy crab soup).

Sweet Things

The Scots are well known for their sweet tooth and a cup of tea or coffee is incomplete without a **shortbread** biscuit. The difference between the factory-made product and home-made shortbread is like chalk and cheese, so do make sure you sample the real thing. If you want to take some home with you, look for the navy blue boxes or tins made by The Shortbread House, on sale in Jenner's, the Waverley Tourist Information Office and elsewhere. **Millionaire's Short-bread**, coated with toffee and chocolate, is over-sweet and cloying.

Two Scots desserts well worth a try are **Atholl Brose**, whipped cream, honey and whisky with oatmeal, and **Cranachan**, a similar mixture of cream and oatmeal but with berries. Two titanically heavy, dark fruit-filled winter confections, not unlike Christmas pudding, are **black bun** and **clootie dumpling**. The former comes in a pastry case, the other is simply boiled in a cloth.

ENJOYING YOUR VISIT

Drinks

The national drink is, of course, **whisky** – the word derives from the Gaelic term *uisge-beatha*, or *uisge beagh*, meaning 'water of life'. In its simplest terms, whisky is made by adding pure Scottish water to malted barley – to get what is known as a single malt whisky – or to a mixture of malted barley and unmalted cereals (such as maize), to achieve a blended or grain whisky. It is then taken through the distillation process and matured in barrels. There are around 2 000 types of

The Scotch Whisky Heritage Centre, on the Royal Mile.

blended whisky but only 100 single malts. Most distilleries are north of Edinburgh, and those in the Highlands, producing single malts are regarded as the best. The **Scotch Whisky Heritage Centre** on the Royal Mile (*see* p.28) will tell you more about the history and process of manufacture.

In traditional pubs you will see a small water fountain/tap on the bar, so that drinkers can add a little drop of water to their whisky. Connoisseurs will tell you that this releases the flavours and is much better than drinking it neat.

Whisky is also the basis for a number of liqueurs, the most famous being **Drambuie**, reputedly the favourite of Bonnie Prince Charlie. The 250-year-old recipe is still a secret but is a blend of up to 18 separate malt whiskies, herbs and heather honey. Try it over ice as an aperitif.

As in England, Scottish **beers** divide broadly into traditional ales and continental-style lagers. The ales, similar to English Bitters, are traditionally graded 60/- (60 shillings), 70/- (also known as Special), 80/- (also known as Heavy) and 90/-, indicating the tax per barrel that was levied in the old days, well before decimal currency. The more shillings, the higher the strength. Both 60/- and 90/- are now rare.

In case you were wondering, it is the hoppy smell of the McEwans mega brewery at Fountainbridge, which often permeates the whole city centre, but their tasteless fizzy keg beers are not recommended. Instead, look out for real ales from independent local breweries such as Belhaven, Caledonia and Broughton.

The national soft drink is the fluorescent orange, teeth-melting Irn-Bru ('made frae girders').

Eating Out

As you would expect from a capital city, you can find cooking from almost every corner of the world in Edinburgh. A few years ago, Scottish food that was both interesting and affordable was a rarity but recently there has been a renaissance of local cuisine, often pairing it with foreign and more modern influences. Think venison steak on thyme-roasted root vegetables, salmon fish cakes with spicy rouille, even haggis in filo pastry! The city also has many fine French restaurants and the 'Auld Alliance' (of Scotland and France) is now also a culinary partnership.

Eating out can be expensive but at lunch times and sometimes early evening many restaurants, even top ones, offer bargain *table d'hôte* menus.

Here is a selection of restaurants, cafés and pubs which capture the spirit of eating and

The Witchery by the Castle.

drinking in Edinburgh. A meal in any of these places should be inexpensive to moderately priced, except where indicated. Telephone numbers are given only where reservations are accepted.

For further reading and suggestions on where to eat, pick up a copy of the excellent *Edinburgh and Glasgow Eating & Drinking Guide*, produced by *The List* and updated annually.

Recommended Restaurants

The Witchery by the Castle *352 Castlehill, Royal Mile* ☎ **0131 225 5613**. Edinburgh's most atmospheric restaurant is set in low, stone, candlelit medieval tenement rooms. If that doesn't grab you, look in to its Secret Garden, an imaginatively restored old school courtyard. Its Scottish gourmet fayre is highly rated. Expensive, but great value fixed-price menus at lunch time and early evening.

Howies *Glanville Place, Stockbridge* ☎ **0131 225 5553**. The Stockbridge branch of this bright and breezy young fashionable chain, serving good Scottish fare with a (slightly) modern twist. Excellent value set price menus; licensed but you can bring your own bottle (corkage charge).

Maison Bleue *36-38 Victoria Street* ☎ **0131 226 1900**. Contemporary cooking from all over the world, amid stone arches and trendy dark decor. The owner is Algerian, so start with the deliciously authentic *chorba* soup. Their lunch time set menu is astonishing value.

Café Royal Oyster Bar *17a West Register Street* ☎ **0131 556 4124.** A city legend, and period-piece dining room replete with marble, stained glass, gilded cornices, gleaming wood and painted tiles. Expensive but a great one-off treat.

Greyfriars Bobby pub, with its loyal namesake outside.

Mussel Inn *61-65 Rose Street* ☎ **0131 225 5979**. Buzzing, trendy, bright and clean, the Mussel Inn serves the best value seafood in the city centre. Go for a large pot of the eponymous bivalves, cooked in all sorts of imaginative ways.

Lancers 5 *Hamilton Place, Stockbridge* ☎ **0131 332 3444**. One of the city's most venerable and popular Indian restaurants, this Stockbridge institution has pleased innumerable locals and visitors, including Billy Connolly and Elton John. Don't miss the gingery chicken murgh, but avoid eating in the front room/bar area.

Pubs

Rose Street used to be the golden mile as far as drinking in Edinburgh was concerned, but today almost all of its pubs have been modernised and aimed at the 18-30 age group, often with disastrous results. If you want to see Edinburgh's pubs as they were 40 years or more ago, try **Mathers** (Queensferry Street, also Broughton Street), the **Bow Bar** (Victoria Street), the **Cumberland Bar** (Cumberland Street) or the **Oxford Bar** (Young Street).

' A good introduction to Edinburgh's pubs is to join the **McEwan's 80/- Edinburgh Literary Pub Tour**, which mixes culture, comedy, a pint or three of 'heavy' and a couple of wee drams to make a very successful evening's cocktail (☎ **0131 226 6665** for details).

Recommended Pubs

Jolly Judge *7a James Court, Lawnmarket*. Easily missed, this cosy, friendly little basement pub is a great place to warm up on a cold winter's day. In summer, you can sit outside in one of the Old Town's nicest closes, adjacent to the Writers' Museum.

The Abbotsford *3 Rose Street*. Wood panelling, a carved painted ceiling, painted tiles and a classic gleaming mahogany 'island bar', liberally stocked with real ales and a multitude of whiskies, are the hallmarks of this classic Edinburgh pub. Along the street, the **Kenilworth** boasts an even more striking interior, but the atmosphere is marred by loud music and a TV screen the size of a small cinema.

Bennet's Bar *8 Leven Street, Tollcross*. Just out of the centre, next to the King's Theatre, this is another Edinburgh drinking institution with a gleaming gantry (drinks counter) groaning under the weight of whisky bottles.

Sheep's Heid Inn *43 The Causeway, Duddingston*. This charming pub, with its very friendly landlady, is claimed to be one of Scotland's oldest hostelries. In summer, its flower-filled courtyard is packed with contented walkers who have just descended from Arthur's Seat.

ENJOYING YOUR VISIT

Theme/character pubs

You might find the following pubs, all devoted to colourful characters or events from Edinburgh's darker side, amusing – at least for as long as it takes to consume a pint: **Mary King's Tavern** (Cockburn Street), **Maggie Dickson's** (Grassmarket), **Jekyll and Hyde** (Hanover Street), **Deacon Brodie's Tavern** (Royal Mile). Most impressive of all is **Frankenstein's**, on the George IV Bridge, though what Mary Shelley's monster has to do with Edinburgh is anyone's guess.

Converted Banks

On George Street, don't miss **The Dome**, which has a cupola that Christopher Wren would have been proud of, and you would be hard pushed to find a more spectacular watering hole. In summer it opens up its leafy garden. A few doors along George Street, **The Standing Order** is another former bank (look for its Fort Knox-like safe door), serving probably the best value real ales and bar food in town.

Recommended Cafés

Edinburgh has a thriving café society, many of them also serving excellent food. Forget the city's numerous Starbucks, Costa and other chain outlets and try some of the following:
Café Hub *Castlehill, Royal Mile.* As

Deacon Brodie's Tavern, on the Royal Mile.

Stylish and creative, the Café Hub.

befits the nerve centre of the Festival, Café Hub is bright, stylish, sophisticated, bohemian and cutting-edge, all rolled into one. The food is inventive, with a foot in every continent. It stages regular food and music events, has outdoor tables, and most importantly, comfy sofas for weary Royal Mile sightseers.

Cornerstone Café *Princes Street.* Take a break from the shopping crowds in this very relaxing, friendly crypt café beneath St John's Church, at the west end of Princes Street. Tables outside in summer. Good vegetarian food served (lunch only).

Patisserie Florentin *8-10 St Giles Street.* A dreamy, friendly Bohemian sort of place, just off the Royal Mile. Perch yourself by the window on the upper floor and enjoy the views.

Elephant House *21 George IV Bridge.* Probably Edinburgh's favourite coffee stop, a home-from-home for students, shoppers and a broad cross-section of locals and visitors. Excellent food, from home-made shortbread to delicious salads and hot snacks. Lovely back room with great views over Greyfriars Churchyard, though it can get smoky.

Number 28 *28 Charlotte Square.* Housed in the National Trust headquarters, there isn't a more elegant place to take tea or coffee in the New Town than this gorgeously restored Georgian house. It's surprisingly light and unfussy, and friendly, too. They also serve good Scottish lunches.

Art Gallery Cafés

Never mind the art, the following cafés all merit a visit in their own right. **Café Newton** at the Dean Gallery; **Café Odile** at the Stills Gallery on Cockburn Street, for a great value three-course French lunch; the **City Art Centre Café**, Market Street, bright and child-friendly; **Queen Street Café** at the Scottish National Portrait Gallery, for tea with Sean Connery – or at least his likeness; the **Gallery Café** at the Scottish National Gallery of Modern Art, for great soups, sandwiches, salads and inventive (mostly) vegetarian food, including a memorable Scottish cheeseboard (in summer, get there early for a patio seat).

ENTERTAINMENT AND NIGHTLIFE

Music

Local musicians play several city centre pubs nightly. For folk and roots music try the **Ensign Ewart** on Castlehill, Royal Mile, **Whistle Binkies** on Niddry Street, **The Hebrides** on Market Street and **Sandy Bells** on Forrest Road. Indie bands play **The Attic** on Dyer's Close, Cowgate, Irish bands do **Finnegan's Wake** on Victoria Street. Jazz fans should beat a path to **Henry's Jazz Bar** on Morrison Street, with live music most nights Wed-Sat. **Cellar No. 1**, at 1 Chambers Street, is another good jazz club.

Queen Street Café, at the Scottish National Portrait Gallery.

Other regular venues, for all kinds of music, include the **Liquid Room** (Victoria Street), **The Venue** (Calton Road), **La Belle Angele** (Hasties Close, Cowgate) and **The Bongo Club** (New Street, Royal Mile). These all double up as night-clubs, changing persona night by night or room by room.

Big names visit **The Edinburgh Playhouse** (18-22 Greenside Place ☎ 0870 606 3424), **Queen's Hall** (Clerk Street ☎ 0131 668 2019), **Usher Hall** (Lothian Road ☎ 0131 228 8616) and the **Corn Exchange** (New Market Road, Gorgie ☎ 0131 443 2437/220 3234) but the mega star turns often prefer to play Glasgow.

Classical Music, Opera, Ballet

Queen's Hall is home to the Edinburgh-based Scottish Chamber Orchestra and the venue for many international name performers. The Royal Scottish National Orchestra (RSNO) is based in Glasgow but plays regularly at the splendid **Usher Hall**.

The striking new 1 900-seat **Edinburgh Festival Theatre** (13-29 Nicolson Street ☎ 0131 529 6000) also stages some classical concerts but is primarily home to Scottish Opera and is used by Scottish Ballet when it is in the capital.

Night-clubs

Edinburgh has a lively club scene, with venues coming into and going out of fashion all the time. There is a bewildering variety of specials and one-nighters going on at any one time, so pick up *The List* and keep your eyes open for flyers in trendy bars and music shops such as Underground Solushun, on Cockburn Street. As well as the clubs listed above, tried and tested venues include **The Vaults** on Niddry Street, **Club Mercado** on Market Street and **Po Na Na** on Frederick Street. Leith is presently a boom area for clubbing. All city clubs close at 3am.

Comedy

The Fringe (*see* p. 94) is the place to catch the best comedians in

Britain but at other times of the year the top venue is **The Stand**, on York Place, with lots of laughs every night and a free Sunday lunch time session.

Theatre

As with comedy, August is the time to see la crème de la crème but throughout the year Edinburgh hosts plenty of top quality stuff to suit all tastes. **The Traverse Theatre** (new writing; on Cambridge Street ☎ 0131 228 1404), the **Edinburgh Playhouse** (touring West End musicals), the **Royal Lyceum** (Grindlay Street, off Lothian Road ☎ 0131 248 4848) and the **King's Theatre** (other popular productions; 2 Leven Street ☎ 0131 529 600) are the main venues. The latter is an Edwardian gem, worth the ticket price alone just to enjoy its lavish interior. In keeping with the city's Fringe tradition, there are also several smaller venues.

Cinema

The home of the International Film Festival in August is **The Filmhouse**, on Lothian Road, so cineastes are sure of a warm welcome year round. **The Lumiere**, at the Royal Museum, and **The Cameo** on Home Street are other favourites for cult and art-house movies. Otherwise there are lots of multiplexes to choose from.

Scottish Evenings

If the idea of a Scottish feast, bagpipes, Highland dancing and other such entertainment appeals, there are two Scottish Evenings in city centre hotels: **George Scottish Evening** at the George Intercontinental (May-early Oct; ☎ 0131 225 1251); and **Hail Caledonia** at the Carlton (May-mid Sept; ☎ 0131 472 3000).

For all the above forms of entertainment, buy a copy of *The List* from any newsagent to see who's on and forthcoming, or pick up a copy of the monthly magazine *What's On* at the Edinburgh and Lothians Tourist Board office.

CHILDREN

While the great architecture, galleries, historical buildings, museums and pubs of the city are mostly for adults, there are plenty of activities for kids too.

Princes Street Gardens are a good place to let off steam, particularly at the west end where there is a good playground. So too is the **Royal Botanic Garden** but for the real outdoors go to **Holyrood Park**.

On the Royal Mile, try the **Camera Obscura**, the **Museum of Childhood**, watch **fudge** being made next door, then nip down Chalmer's Close opposite to do some **brass rubbing**. At the foot of the Mile, **Our Dynamic Earth** is great for all the family.

There are several options just out of the centre. A **boat trip** on *The Maid of the Forth* to Inchcolm Island; its little beach and seal spotting are winners on a warm day. **Butterfly and Insect World** and the **Birds of Prey Centre**, at Lasswade, are deservedly popular, and will be even better when the new £2 million pyramid glasshouse, with lush rainforest and exotic inhabitants, is complete. Two other tried and trusted major attractions are **Deep Sea World** and **Edinburgh Zoo**.

On the ghost theme, try **Witchery Tours** (☎ 0131 225 6745) for a gentle fright; hard-boiled teens will enjoy the **Edinburgh Dungeon** and the **City of the Dead Tour**.

June is a particularly good time to visit, when the **Scottish International Children's Festival** (theatre, film, music, art and dance events) takes place. For events and activities year-round, see the Kids' page in *The List*.

SHOPPING

Edinburgh is an excellent shopping city, with hundreds of independent shops providing friendly personalised service and many individual and unique purchases. The great irony is that many visitors venture no further than **Princes Street**, which is now almost completely lined with bland chainstores. The only real top quality Scottish shop along here is **Jenner's** department store, the world's oldest independent store, established in 1838. Do look into its Great Hall. **Harvey Nichols** is set to provide some competition, opening in Autumn 2002 in a new shopping development on St Andrew Square.

George Street has now taken the grand mantle that Princes Street once held, with some very fine upmarket shops, including **Justerini and Brooks** (wines and whisky), **Crombie Retail** (Crombie coats), **Neal's Yard**

Jenner's department store.

Remedies (alternative lotions and potions), **Penhaligons** (perfumery), **Hamilton and Inches** (jewellery) and **James Thin** (books).

The Royal Mile, once berated for its tourist tat, also boasts many high quality outlets. Tartan and woollens naturally predominate, but also look out for **Royal Mile Whiskies**, **The Cigar Box**, and at the top end of Canongate three beautiful women's knitwear shops: **Ragamuffin**, **Koshka** and **Frontiers**.

Just off the top of the Mile, **Victoria Street/Westbow** is a delightful old-fashioned shopping row, including **Robert Cresser's** 125-year-old brushes and brooms store, **Ian Mellis Cheesemonger**, **Azteca** (South American items), **Pine and Old Lace**, and **Halibut and Herring** (bathroom oddities). Below, leading off Grassmarket, **Cowgatehead**

Gift shop in the Lawnmarket.

features more idiosyncratic delights, including **Mr Wood's Fossils** and **Wind Things** (kites etc.). For more esoteric offerings off the Mile, try **Cockburn Street**.

If you're after food and drink, you can't beat the Mediterranean delights of city legends **Valvona and Crolla** (Elm Row, Leith Walk), or **Peckham's** deli-grocery (Bruntsfield Place). Pick up a famous MacSween's haggis here (also on sale in Jenner's).

Out of town, you can watch lead crystal glass being blown and cut inside the factory at the excellent **Edinburgh Crystal** visitor centre in Penicuik, then visit their extensive shop (free buses from Waverley Station).

SPORT

Edinburgh is not renowned as a sporting city but there is certainly a passion for **football** (soccer), with the city split between Heart of Midlothian ('Hearts') and Hibernian ('Hibs'), who both play in the Scottish Premier League. One of them is usually at home on Saturday afternoon; see the local press or *The List* for details.

Murrayfield Stadium (Corstophine Road ☎ 0131 346 5000) is the home of the Scotland **Rugby Union** national team and, when Scotland are at home during the Six Nations Championship, the city's bars and hotels heave with visiting supporters.

The stadium is also home to the Scottish Claymores **American football** team.

Just out of town (10km/6 miles east, on Linkfield Road ☎ 0131 665 2859), Musselburgh Racecourse is Scotland's oldest **horse-racing** course.

In summer, you can catch national or international **athletics** meetings at Meadowbank Sports Stadium, just on the outskirts of town (139 London Road ☎ 0131 661 5351).

Edinburgh's Royal Commonwealth Pool (21 Dalkeith Road ☎ 0131 667 7211) is an Olympic-sized **swimming** pool open for both serious lane-bashing and messing about on water slides.

Golf courses, not surprisingly, are plentiful. There are over 20 within the city limits alone and dozens more within easy reach, including Muirfield, host to the British Open Championship in 2002, and Dalmahoy. The tourist information office can help with details and supply a discounted golf pass; otherwise click on www.edinburgh.org/golf.

Skiers and would-be skiers might like to note that Europe's longest **dry-ski slope** (measuring 400m) lies just south of the city, at Hillend (Midlothian Ski Centre ☎ 0131 445 4433). It enjoys some great views.

In winter, a romantic open-air **ice skating** rink is created in Princes Street Gardens.

THE BASICS

Before You Go
Visitors entering Scotland from any country other than the United Kingdom should have a full passport valid for the period of their stay. No visa is required for USA, Canadian, Australian, New Zealand or EU nationals. Other nationalities should check before travelling. No vaccinations are necessary.

Getting There
By Air
Edinburgh Airport is 12km (8 miles) west of the city and handles domestic and international flights, including direct flights to Paris and transatlantic charters (☎ 0131 333 1000). British Airways (☎ 08457 222 111) is the national carrier and flies regularly to Edinburgh from Heathrow, as does British Midland (☎ 0870 6070 555) which is usually cheaper. Easyjet (☎ 0870 6000 000) flies from Luton. Flight time from London is about an hour.

A special Airlink 100 bus service runs every 10 minutes during the day between the airport and city centre (Waverley Bridge) and takes around 25 minutes. Buy your tickets on board (£3.30 one way, £5 return). Taxis are available (☎ 0131 344 3344) but are expensive, costing around £15 for the journey between the airport and Princes Street.

By Train
Edinburgh has two main railway stations: Waverley and Haymarket. Great North Eastern Railway (GNER) (☎ 08457 225 225) serves the east coast of mainland Britain, with a fast, comfortable, efficient service from London, King's Cross to Edinburgh (Waverley Station) taking around 4 hours. Virgin Trains (☎ 08457 484 950) run from London (Euston Station) to Edinburgh (Haymarket Station) but with a change at Birmingham. The total journey time is around 5½ to 6 hours. From Haymarket to the west end of Princes Street is a 10-minute walk (bus no 3, 3A, 12 or 25).

By Coach
National Express operate a regular coach service to Edinburgh from London and other towns and cities in England and Wales; for further information ☎ 0990 80 80 80.
Scottish Citylink serves towns within Scotland; for further information ☎ 0990 50 50 50. All coaches arrive at the St Andrew Square Bus Station, Clyde Street, Edinburgh EH1 3DU.

He who pays the piper calls the tune.

A-Z

Accidents and Breakdowns

Contact the rental firm in the event of an accident or break-down. It is obligatory to carry a red warning triangle or to have hazard warning lights to use if you break down. If you have an accident, exchange names, addresses and insurance details. In an emergency ☎ 999.
See also **Driving, Emergencies**

Accommodation see p.96

Airports see Getting There, p.112

Banks

Bank opening hours are variable but minimum opening hours are 9am-4pm; some branches open until 5.30pm and also on Saturday mornings. Smaller branches may close at lunch time. Exchange bureaux stay open longer but give a less favourable rate of exchange. ATM cash-dispensing machines can be found all over the city centre. Some form of identifica-tion is required when changing travellers' cheques.

Bicycles

Bicycle hire is not recommended for inexperienced cyclists as city centre traffic can be heavy, and the cobbles and hills can make cycling hard work. There is, however, a good network of cycle paths; an old railway line has been converted to a safe flat cycle route near Stockbridge; The Water of Leith Walkway (*see* p.72) is another pleasant traffic-free option, albeit rather narrow in parts. So if you are a keen urban cyclist, contact Spokes (☎ 0131 313 2114), the local cycle lobby group who produce excellent cycling maps of the city and surrounding area. Hire companies include BikeTrax (☎ 0131 228 6633), Edinburgh Bicycle Co-operative (☎ 0131 228 1368) and Edinburgh Cycle Hire (☎ 0131 556 5560).

Breakdowns see Accidents

Camping

The nearest official site to the city centre is at Silverknowes (Marine Drive ☎ 0131 312 6874) 5km (3½ miles) northwest of the city. There is a direct bus service into town from outside the camp site. Contact the Tourist Information Office for other sites.

Car Hire

There are numerous car hire agencies, both at the airport and in town. The rates are among the highest in Europe but local firms are usually significantly cheaper than international operators.

A full list of car hire firms is available from the Tourist Information Office, or in Yellow Pages.

Below is a selection:

Avis 100 Dalry Road, Haymarket
☎ 0131 337 6363

Budget 111 Glasgow Road
☎ 08457 606 6669

Capital Car & Van Hire
101 Easter Road
☎ 0131 652 9898

Edinburgh Car & Van Hire
Saughton Mains Street
☎ 0131 443 3366

Edinburgh Self Drive 45 Lochrin
Place ☎ 0131 229 8686

Europcar 24 East London Street
☎ 0131 557 3456

Hertz Waverley Station
☎ 0131 557 5272

The minimum age limit is generally 23 and in most cases you must have held a full licence for at least two years. Make sure that collision damage waiver is included in the insurance.

See also **Driving, Accidents and Breakdowns**

Churches *see* **Religion**

Climate *see* p.91

Clothing

Pack warm clothes for winter and even in summer you should bring a light jacket and jumper as nights can be cool. As the weather is unpredictable, it is best to dress in layers and at any time of year be prepared for rain, which may be sustained in

Detail of the Ross Fountain.

winter and showery in spring and summer. If you are cold, there is no shortage of high-quality Scottish woollens to keep you warm.

Casual wear is the norm, although you will look out of place at Edinburgh's smarter restaurants and hotel dining rooms unless you have made an effort.

Most clothing measurements are standard throughout Europe but differ from those in the UK and the USA. The following are examples:

Women's sizes

UK	8	10	12	14	16	18
Europe	38	40	42	44	46	48
US	6	8	10	12	14	16

Women's shoes

UK	4.5	5	5.5	6	6.5	7
Europe	38	38	39	39	40	41
US	6	6.5	7	7.5	8	8.5

Men's suits

UK/US	36	38	40	42	44	46
Europe	46	48	50	52	54	56

Men's shirts

UK/US	14	14.5	15	15.5	16	16.5	17
Europe	36	37	38	39/40	41	42	43

Men's shoes

UK	7	7.5	8.5	9.5	10.5	11
Europe	41	42	43	44	45	46
US	8	8.5	9.5	10.5	11.5	12

Consulates and Embassies

Australia
25 Bernard Street, Leith, Edinburgh EH6 6SH
☎ 0131 555 4500
fax 0131 554 3051

Canada
3 George Street, Edinburgh EH2 2XZ ☎ **0131 220 4333**
USA
3 Regent Terrace, Calton Hill, Edinburgh EH7 5BW
☎ **0131 556 8315**
fax 0131 557 6023

Crime

The centre of Edinburgh is, by and large, a safe place for visitors, though after dark do stick to the main, well-lit streets. You should take the usual precautions, and beware of pickpockets in crowded places such as Princes Street on a Saturday, and many central places during the Festival. Be careful where you put your bags in pubs, cafés and restaurants.

Avoid walking in city parks, such as the Meadows, after dark, and keep away from Cowgate and Grassmarket late at night if you want to avoid booze-fuelled youths.

If you have a car, try to park it in a secured garage or space, and do not leave any valuables inside.

Currency see Money

Customs and Entry Regulations

There are no restrictions on goods brought into Scotland from EU countries, though limits apply to other countries. For goods taken out of the country, the normal EU regulations apply to EU residents: 200 cigarettes or 100 cigarillos or 250g (8.8oz) of tobacco; 2 litres still table wine plus 1 litre spirits (over 22% abv) or 2 litres fortified wine (under 22% abv), sparkling wine or other liqueurs; 60ml perfumes; 250 ml toilet water; other goods to the value of £75 for EU citizens, £145 non-EU citizens.

USA and Canadian citizens may take home up to $400 and $300 worth of goods respectively, as well as their tobacco allowances.

There are no restrictions on taking currency into or out of the UK.

Disabled Visitors

For guides to facilities and accommodation services contact RADAR, 12 City Forum, 250 City Road, London EC1V 8AF ☎ **(020) 7250 3222**; or the Holiday Care Service, 2 Old Bank Chambers, Station Road, Horley, Surrey RH6 9HW ☎ **(01293) 774 535**.

In Edinburgh, contact the Lothian Coalition of Disabled People, Norton Park, 57 Albion Road, Edinburgh EH7 5QY ☎ **0131 475 2360** fax 0131 475 2392, who publish the free *Access Guide to Edinburgh*.

Driving

For visitors not used to the European style of relatively fast driving along narrow roads, driving in Edinburgh may well be intimidating. As, however, the town is easily explored on foot, you certainly don't need a car and it would be more of a liability than an asset. Street parking is always difficult and clamping or tow-away regulations are strictly enforced, though most hotels have some parking provision. Most excursions are well covered by public transport and private coach excursions. If, however, you wish to explore the Borders or Fife in more detail, then a car is the best option.

Traffic outside Edinburgh is relatively light. Remember that

Heraldic panel, Holyroodhouse Palace.

the basic rules of the road are drive on the left and give way to traffic coming from the right. Road surfaces are good.

Petrol stations are frequent in and around the city but don't venture into the countryside running on low as they can be few and far between on the smaller roads. Petrol stations are open daily; petrol is much more expensive than in the USA.

The following speed limits apply: 110kph/70mph on motorways; 100kph/60mph on all out of town roads; 50-64kph/30-40mph in towns, and as posted. Note that speed limit signs are posted in miles per hour.

Seat belts are compulsory. *See also* **Accidents and Breakdowns**

Electric Current

The voltage in Scotland is 220/240V. Plugs and sockets are of the square-fitting three-pin variety.

Embassies see Consulates

Emergencies

For all emergency services (police, ambulance and fire) ☎ 999. These calls are free.

Etiquette

The Scots are generally a friendly, easy-going people and there is little in the way of formal etiquette to worry about.

Remember that most Scots are very patriotic, so never say anything that may be interpreted as belittling the country, particularly in comparison with England. The term 'Scotch' is generally used only of whisky. The correct term for a Scotsman or Scotswoman is 'Scottish' or 'Scots'.

Guidebooks see Maps

Health

Edinburgh has a proud record of medical break-throughs and medical university teaching, and the standard of health care is first class. In theory, EU residents can take advantage of the reciprocal free medical treatment arrangement, provided that a completed E111 form is held. In practice, you may end up paying for it and then claiming a refund at home. Be sure to keep all receipts to support your claim. An E111 is not necessary for UK residents, and accident and emergency treatment is free to all. The Royal Infirmary of Edinburgh, 1 Lauriston Place ☎ 0131 536 4000 provides a 24-hour service.

Non-EU residents are charged for all non-emergency treatment and it is vital to have holiday insurance which covers this eventuality.

Hours see Opening Hours

Information see **Tourist Information Offices**

Language

Although it has many words and sayings of its own, Scottish is basically a dialect of the English language. The Edinburgh accent is much softer and more intelligible to visitors than that of other parts of Scotland. Below are a few Scottish words that you may encounter.

Lost Property

Report the loss of any valuable item to the police and keep a note of their reference number for any subsequent insurance claim.

Airport ☎ 0131 344 386
Bus (Lothian Regional Transport) ☎ 0131 554 4492
Railway Stations ☎ 0131 556 2477
Taxis ☎ 0131 311 3141

---

auld / old (the Auld Alliance is with the French; the Auld Enemy generally refers to England!)

bonnie / pretty, beautiful

burn / stream

ceilidh (pronounced *caley*) / gathering for Scots/Gaelic singing, dancing and story-telling

clan / family or Highland tribe

couthy (pronounced *coo-thee*) / nice, pleasant

douce / mild, gentle, kind (also used of pleasant weather)

dram / measure (of whisky)

dreich (pronounced *dreech*, with a hard *ch*) / dull, wet, miserable, of weather

glen / Highland valley

ken / know (as in, d'ye ken … ? / do you know … ?)

kirk / church

laird / lord

laddie / boy

lassie / girl

Sassenach / non-Scot (usually perjorative, of English people)

see you! / Hey! (to attract attention)

wee / small

wynd / narrow alleyway between houses

Maps and Guidebooks

The *Michelin Red Guide Great Britain and Ireland* contains detailed information on hotels and restaurants throughout Scotland, including Edinburgh. The *Michelin Green Guide Scotland* has information on the main sights and attractions in Edinburgh, detailed street maps of the city and also includes other towns and attractions you may visit as excursions from Edinburgh. The *Michelin Road Map 401 Scotland* (1:400 000) will help with route-planning. If you are staying for only a few days and don't want to venture out of the centre, the excellent *Edinburgh Navigator City Centre Pocket Map* (free from the Waverley Tourist Information Office) is perfectly adequate. Also ask at the tourist office for a bus map.

Money

The monetary unit is the pound sterling, £. Although notes and some coins have Scottish designs and emblems, they are legal tender throughout the United Kingdom. Notes come in denominations of £5, £10, £20 and £50; coins come in 1p, 2p, 5p, 10p, 20p, 50p, £1 and £2.

All major credit cards are accepted in most city centre establishments. Hotels and many large shops will also accept travellers' cheques, though you may be charged at a less favourable rate of exchange.

There are no restrictions on the import and export of currency. Banks and exchange bureaux can be found at the airport and all over the city. *See also* **Banks**

Newspapers

Scotland has its own newspapers – of the quality papers, *The Scotsman* is published in Edinburgh, *The Herald* in Glasgow – as well as regional editions of the main English papers. The *Evening News* is a tabloid covering

Thistle architectural detail.

local Edinburgh news, while the tabloid *Daily Record* covers all of Scotland. *Scotland on Sunday* is perhaps the best of the heavies. Foreign newspapers are on sale at various city centre newsagents; try International Newsagents, at 351 High Street, Royal Mile. For events listings, see *The List* (on sale fortnightly) or *What's On* (monthly).

Opening Hours

Shops: Traditional shop hours are Mon-Sat 9/9.30am-5.30/6pm, with late opening (until 7.30/8pm) on Thursday. A good number of shops now open on a Sunday afternoon also.

Chemists: These open traditional shop hours, with a rota system ensuring at least one chemist per neighbourhood is open late in case of emergencies (its address is posted in the window of the other chemists and is also listed in *The Scotsman*. Boots, 48 Shandwick Place, New Town is open late: Mon-Fri 8am-9pm, Sat 8am-7pm, Sun 10am-5pm.

Pubs/bars: Each licensed premises has its own opening hours but most have all-day licensing (11am-11pm). As a minimum you can count on pubs being open to 11pm; some open until 3am, as local regulations dictate that all pubs, bars and nightclubs must close at 3am.

Museums: Normal opening hours are Mon-Sat around 10am-5/6pm, and Sun 2pm-5/6pm.

Note that during the Festival (throughout August) most Edinburgh establishments, particularly pubs and bars, open longer hours.

Police

Scottish police officers wear flat peaked hats with a black-and-white chequered band. They are invariably friendly and approachable. The main station is at Fettes Avenue, EH14 ☎ **0131 311 3377**. In emergency ☎ **999**.

Post Offices

Post Offices are usually open Mon-Fri 9am-5.30pm and Sat 9am-12.30pm. The main St James Post Office, in the St James Centre, is open Mon 9am-5.30pm, Tue-Fri 8.30am-5.30pm and Sat 8.30am-6pm. There are two other main central offices in the New Town, on Frederick Street and Hope Street.

Stamps may be bought at newsagents displaying a red postal sign in the window, in some supermarkets and other shops, as well as at post offices. It costs 37p to send a letter (up to 20g) or postcard to EU countries. Post boxes are painted red.

Poste restante mail should be

addressed to the person, Poste Restante, Hope Street Post Office, 7 Hope Street, Edinburgh EH2 4EN.

Public Holidays

New Year: 1 & 2 January
Good Friday: variable
Easter Monday: variable
May Day: First Monday in May
Victoria Day (Edinburgh only): third Monday in May
Spring Bank Holiday Monday: Last Monday in May
Summer Bank Holiday: First Monday in August
Autumn Holiday (Edinburgh only): Third Monday in September
St Andrew's Day: 30 November
Christmas Day: 25 December
Boxing Day: 26 December

Tweeddale Court, off the High Street on the Royal Mile.

Religion

Most widespread is the Church of Scotland, which is Presbyterian (a form of Protestantism). There are also many Roman Catholic, Episcopalian, Baptist and other churches (often splinter groups of the main denominations), as well as religions other than Christian. Enquire at the Tourist Information Office for addresses and times of services.

Smoking

Smoking is banned in most public places.

Taxis see Transport

Telephones

Public telephones can be used to call anywhere in the world. They accept coins, credit cards or telephone cards, available from newsagents in denominations of £2-10.

Cheap rates apply Mon-Fri 8pm-8am and all weekend.
For operator ☎ 100
For international operator
    ☎ 155
For local directory enquiries
    ☎ 192
For international directory
    enquiries ☎ 153
Country codes are as follows:
Australia ☎ 00 61
Canada ☎ 00 1
New Zealand ☎ 00 64
USA ☎ 00 1

To call Edinburgh from abroad ☎ 00 44 131

Time Difference

Scotland is on GMT in winter; from late March until late October the clocks go forward one hour, so that it is usually one hour behind the rest of Europe. It is five hours ahead of US Eastern Standard Time.

Tipping

If a service charge is not included in the restaurant bill, and the service and food have been good, then leave a tip of around 10 per cent. It is also customary to tip the hotel-room maid 50p-£1 per day. A good tour guide deserves a tip of £1-2 (depending on the length of the tour), and a polite and helpful taxi driver should also be given a tip of around 10 per cent. Porters, doormen, bellhops and so on should be given anywhere between 50p and £2, depending on the service performed.

It is not customary to tip bartenders in cash. If you want to show your appreciation, offer them a drink instead (don't be offended if they take the cash equivalent).

Tourist Information Offices

The **Scottish Tourist Board**'s head office is at 23 Ravelston Terrace, Edinburgh EH4 3EU ☎ **0131 332 2433** fax 0131 459

2434 www.holiday.scotland.net

The **British Tourist Authority (BTA)** can help with planning a trip to Scotland, and have offices abroad:

USA
625 North Michigan Ave, Suite 1510, Chicago, Illinois 60611
☎ 312 787 0490
551 5th Avenue, Suite 701, New York, NY 10176 ☎ 212 986 2266
Canada
111 Avenue Rd, Suite 450, Toronto, Ontario, M5R 3J8
☎ 416 961 8124
Australia
210 Clarence St, Sydney, NSW 2000 ☎ 612 267 4666

Once you get to Edinburgh, the **Edinburgh & Scotland Information Centre**, above Waverley Station, 3 Princes Street, is a good place to begin your visit. As well as general information, they also deal with accommodation reservations, tours, excursions, coach tickets, theatres and Scottish entertainments. Try to go first thing in the morning as it gets very busy.

The centre's opening hours are: winter, Mon-Wed 9am-5pm, Thu-Sat 9am-6/7pm, Sun 10am-5/6pm; summer, Mon-Sat 9am-7pm, Sun 10am-7pm. These are extended during the Festival. ☎ 0131 473 3800 fax 0131 473 3881 www.edinburgh.org
For booking accommodation in advance, e-mail: centres@eltb.org

The other Edinburgh office is at the airport (open daily all year) ☎ 0131 333 1000 fax 0131 335 3576.

Representatives of the tourist office also take to the streets wearing distinctive tartan jackets or bright yellow waterproofs; they can be seen at major arrival points and areas of interest, including the Royal Mile, Waverley Bridge and Princes Street.

Tours

There are all sorts of walking tours and bus tours within and outside the city. For an overview take an open-top hop-bus tour with commentary, which allows you to hop on and off at will: **Guide Friday** (133-135 Canongate, Royal Mile ☎ 0131 556 2244) or **Edinburgh Tour – City Sightseeing** (☎ 0131 555 6363) – buses for both depart from Waverley Bridge.

Typically Edinburgh tours that will get you into the spirit of the city, in more ways than one, include the **McEwans 80/- Literary Pub Tour** (*see* p.103) or one of the city's many ghost tours (*see* pp.66-67).

For details of all of these and of coach tours which take you to places of interest outside Edinburgh, enquire at the main tourist office.

Transport

Edinburgh is a compact city and the quickest way to get about the centre is often to walk. Consider a car only for touring outside the city (*see also* **Driving**).

Buses

The public bus service is run by several operators, of whom the biggest is **Lothian Regional Transport (LRT)**. LRT buses (maroon and white) require the correct money, though some of the other operators do give change. **Daysaver tickets** (£2.20 for a day's unlimited travel) will generally make a saving after more than two journeys, and also save you the hassle of handling cash. They are sold on board or at Travelshops. Note, however, that they are not transferable between different bus companies. A weekly, fortnightly or monthly **Ridacard ticket** is a bargain, if you are going to make several regular LRT trips. To get one you will have to take along a passport photo to one of their Travelshops (at Hanover Street and Waverley Bridge). Another option is the **Touristcard** (2–7 days) which costs more but also includes the Edinburgh Classic (sightseeing) Tour and gives discounts on attractions and restaurants.

Hop aboard a colourful tour bus to take in the city sights.

Nightbuses run from around midnight to 4am.

For all bus enquiries pick up a free route map from the tourist office, call into a Travelshop, or call ☎ **0800 232323**.

Taxis
These can be pre-booked, taken from a taxi rank or hailed on the street. The licensed black taxi cabs work on the meter and are expensive. Unlicensed 'minicabs', which are any other form of taxi, are cheaper and generally agree the fare in advance, but get a recommendation to make sure you have an honest and reputable driver. Look in the local directory for a full list of numbers.

TV and Radio
Scotland receives all UK TV channels, to which it introduces a regional element with home-produced shows, and also has its own Scottish Television Channel (STV). Most hotels of a reasonable standard also provide a wide choice of satellite and/or cable channels.

In addition to the UK-wide radio channels, BBC Radio Scotland (92.4-94.7FM) and the local station Radio Forth (97.3FM) are also worth a listen.

Vaccinations see **Before You Go, p.112**

Water
The tap water is perfectly safe to drink.

The ceiling of the Thistle Chapel, in St Giles' Cathedral.

INDEX

INDEX